The Witnesses

OF THE

BOOK OF MORMON

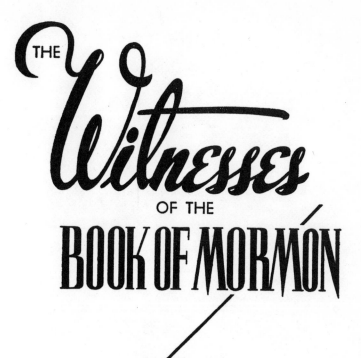

THE Witnesses OF THE BOOK OF MORMÓN

COMPILED by PRESTON NIBLEY

DESERET BOOK COMPANY
Salt Lake City, Utah
1973

ISBN No. 0-87747-308-0

Lithographed by

DESERET NEWS PRESS

in the United States of America

FOREWORD

In compiling this volume, special effort has been made to gather all the information that is available regarding the Three Witnesses of the Book of Mormon, their great vision, their testimonies of the event and also the circumstances which led to the testimony of the Eight Witnesses.

Including the Prophet Joseph Smith, there were Twelve Witnesses of the validity of the Sacred Record. As the Prophet was the principal witness, it has been thought proper to add several important documents which were written or dictated by him. Short sketches of the lives of the Eleven Witnesses and statements of various persons who were acquainted with them and their activities have also been included.

In reading this volume it will be noticed that minor discrepancies occur in the narrations of the witnesses as to the manner in which the Book of Mormon was translated. For the correct answer to all questions the reader should be referred to the accounts given by the Prophet Joseph Smith.

Much of the information contained in this volume would not have been available except for the persistence, foresight and indefatigable labors of that great gatherer of Mormon history, Andrew Jenson, who, as early as 1888, visited the scenes of the activities of the Witnesses and interviewed many people who were personally acquainted with them. These observations he recorded with meticulous care and later published in his *L. D. S. Biographical Encyclopedia* and *Historical Record*.

It is my hope that this volume will be useful to students of our Church history and that the information it contains may inspire greater faith in the Book of Mormon and in the divine mission of the Prophet Joseph Smith.

PRESTON NIBLEY.

Salt Lake City, Utah
November 30, 1953

v

CONTENTS

PART FOUR

Martin Harris

PART FIVE

Short sketches of the lives of the Eight Witnesses of the Book of Mormon

PART SIX

Miscellaneous Documents

Part One

★ ★ ★

Verses in the Doctrine and Covenants, and Book of Mormon, and statements by the Prophet Joseph Smith and others regarding the Witnesses of the Book of Mormon

I

VERSES IN THE DOCTRINE AND COVENANTS PERTAINING TO THE WITNESSES OF THE BOOK OF MORMON

The first mention that there should be Three Witnesses to the coming forth of the Book of Mormon is found in a revelation given to the Prophet Joseph Smith in March, 1829. (Doctrine and Covenants 5:9-15)

This revelation was given after the 116 pages of the Book of Mormon had been recorded by Martin Harris, and before Oliver Cowdery had begun to act as Joseph's scribe.

BEHOLD, VERILY I SAY UNTO YOU, I have reserved those things which I have entrusted unto you, my servant Joseph, for a wise purpose in me, and it shall be made known unto future generations;

But this generation shall have my word through you;

And in addition to your testimony, the testimony of three of my servants, whom I shall call and ordain, unto whom I will show these things, and they shall go forth with my words that are given through you.

Yea, they shall know of a surety that these things are true, for from heaven will I declare it unto them.

I will give them power that they may behold and view these things as they are;

And to none else will I grant this power, to receive this same testimony among this generation, in this the beginning of the rising up and the coming forth of my church out of the wilderness — clear as the moon, and fair as the sun, and terrible as an army with banners.

And the testimony of three witnesses will I send forth of my word.

II

ACCOUNT BY JOSEPH SMITH IN
CHURCH HISTORY

In the History of the Church, vol. 1, page 52, we have the account of the vision of the Three Witnesses, as written or dictated by the Prophet Joseph Smith himself. The events related took place in June, 1829.

IN THE COURSE of the work of translation, we ascertained that three special witnesses were to be provided by the Lord, to whom He would grant that they should see the plates from which this work (the Book of Mormon) should be translated; and that these witnesses should bear record of the same, as will be found recorded, Book of Mormon, page 581 (Book of Ether 5:2-4), and also page 86 (II Nephi 11:3). Almost immediately after we had made this discovery, it occurred to Oliver Cowdery, David Whitmer, and the aforementioned Martin Harris (who had come to inquire after our progress in the work) that they would have me inquire of the Lord to know if they might not obtain of Him the privilege to be these three special witnesses; and finally they became so very solicitous, and urged me so much to inquire that at length I complied; and through the Urim and Thummim, I obtained of the Lord for them the following:

REVELATION, *to Oliver Cowdery, David Whitmer, and Martin Harris, at Fayette, Seneca County, New York, June 1829, given previous to their viewing the Plates containing the Book of Mormon.*

1. Behold, I say unto you, that you must rely upon my word, which if you do with full purpose of heart, you shall have a view of the plates, and also of the breastplate, the sword of Laban, the Urim and Thummim, which were given to the brother of Jared upon the mount, when he talked with the Lord face to face, and the miraculous directors which were given to Lehi while in the wilderness, on the borders of the Red Sea.

2. And it is by your faith that you shall obtain a view of them, even by that faith which was had by the prophets of old.

3. And after that you have obtained faith, and have seen them with your eyes, you shall testify of them, by the power of God;

4. And this you shall do that my servant Joseph Smith, Jun., may not be destroyed, that I may bring about my righteous purposes unto the children of men in this work.

5. And ye shall testify that you have seen them, even as my servant Joseph Smith, Jun., has seen

them; for it is by my power that he has seen them, and it is because he had faith.

6. And he has translated the book, even that part which I have commanded him, and as your Lord and your God liveth it is true.

7. Wherefore, you have received the same power, and the same faith, and the same gift like unto him;

8. And if you do these last commandments of mine, which I have given you, the gates of hell shall not prevail against you; for my grace is sufficient for you, and you shall be lifted up at the last day.

9. And I, Jesus Christ, your Lord and your God, have spoken it unto you, that I might bring about my righteous purposes unto the children of men. Amen.

Not many days after the above commandment was given, we four, viz., Martin Harris, David Whitmer, Oliver Cowdery and myself, agreed to retire into the woods, and try to obtain, by fervent and humble prayer, the fulfillment of the promises given in the above revelation — that they should have a view of the plates. We accordingly made choice of a piece of woods convenient to Mr. Whitmer's house, to which we retired, and having knelt down, we began to pray in much faith to Almighty God to bestow upon us a realization of these promises.

According to previous arrangement, I commenced by vocal prayer to our Heavenly Father, and was followed by each of the others in succession.

We did not at the first trial, however, obtain any answer or manifestation of divine favor in our behalf. We again observed the same order of prayer, each calling on and praying fervently to God in rotation, but with the same result as before.

Upon this, our second failure, Martin Harris proposed that he should withdraw himself from us, believing, as he expressed himself, that his presence was the cause of our not obtaining what we wished for. He accordingly withdrew from us, and we knelt down again, and had not been many minutes engaged in prayer, when presently we beheld a light above us in the air, of exceeding brightness; and behold, an angel stood before us. In his hands he held the plates which we had been praying for these to have a view of. He turned over the leaves one by one, so that we could see them, and discern the engravings thereon distinctly. He then addressed himself to David Whitmer, and said, "David, blessed is the Lord, and he that keeps His commandments;" when, immediately afterwards, we heard a voice from out of the bright light above us, saying, "These plates have been revealed by the power of God, and they have been translated by the power of God. The translation of them which you have seen is correct, and I command you to bear record of what you now see and hear."

I now left David and Oliver, and went in pursuit of Martin Harris, whom I found at a considerable distance, fervently engaged in prayer. He soon told me, however, that he had not yet prevailed with the Lord, and earnestly requested me to join him in prayer, that he also might realize the same blessings which we had just received. We accordingly joined in prayer, and ultimately obtained our desires, for before we had yet finished, the same vision was opened to our view, at least it was again opened to me, and I once more beheld and heard the same things; whilst at the same moment, Martin Harris cried out, apparently in an ecstasy of joy, " 'Tis enough; 'tis enough; mine eyes have beheld; mine eyes have beheld;" and jumping up, he shouted, "Hosanna," blessing God, and otherwise rejoiced exceedingly.

Having thus, through the mercy of God, obtained these glorious manifestations, it now remained for these three individuals to fulfill the commandment which they had received, viz., to bear record of these things; in order to accomplish which, they drew up and subscribed the following document:

THE TESTIMONY OF THREE WITNESSES

Be it known unto all nations, kindreds, tongues, and people, unto whom this work shall come: That we, through the grace of God the Father, and our Lord Jesus Christ, have seen the plates which contain this record, which is a record of the people of Nephi, and also of the Lamanites, their brethren, and also of the people of Jared, who came from the tower of which hath been spoken. And we also know that they have been translated by the gift and power of God, for His voice hath declared it unto us; wherefore we know of a surety that the work is true. And we also testify that we have seen the engravings which are upon the plates; and they have been shown unto us by the power of God, and not of man. And we declare with words of soberness, that an angel of God came down from heaven, and he brought and laid before our eyes, that we beheld and saw the plates, and the engravings thereon; and we know that it is by the grace of God the Father, and our Lord Jesus Christ, that we beheld and bear record that these things are true. And it is marvelous in our eyes. Nevertheless, the voice of the Lord commanded us that we should bear record of it; wherefore, to be obedient unto the commandments of God, we bear testimony of these things. And we know that if we are faithful in Christ, we shall rid our garments of the blood of all men, and be found spotless before the judgment-seat of Christ, and shall dwell with him eternally in the heavens. And the honor be to the Father, and to the Son, and to the Holy Ghost, which is one God. Amen.

Oliver Cowdery

David Whitmer

Martin Harris

Soon after these things had transpired, the following additional testimony was obtained:

THE TESTIMONY OF EIGHT WITNESSES

Be it known unto all nations, kindreds, tongues, and people, unto whom this work shall come: That Joseph Smith, Jun., the translator of this work, has shown unto us the plates of which hath been spoken, which have the appearance of gold; and as many of the leaves as the said Smith has translated, we did handle with our hands; and we also saw the engravings thereon, all of which has the appearance of ancient work, and of curious workmanship. And this we bear record, with words of soberness, that the said Smith has shown unto us, for we have seen and hefted, and know of a surety that the said Smith has got the plates of which we have spoken. And we give our names unto the world to witness unto the world that we have seen. And we lie not, God bearing witness of it.

Christian Whitmer   *Hiram Page*
Jacob Whitmer   *Joseph Smith, Sen.*
Peter Whitmer, Jun.   *Hyrum Smith*
John Whitmer   *Samuel H. Smith*

III

VERSES IN THE BOOK OF MORMON WHICH REFER TO THE THREE WITNESSES

The verses in the Book of Mormon, referred to by the Prophet Joseph Smith, which encouraged Oliver Cowdery, David Whitmer and Martin Harris to ask the Lord in prayer that they might be privileged to be the Three Witnesses, are as follows:

AND BEHOLD, ye may be privileged that ye may show the plates unto those who shall assist to bring forth this work:

And unto three shall they be shown by the power of God; wherefore they shall know of a surety that these things are true.

And in the mouth of three witnesses shall these things be established; and the testimony of three, and this work, in the which shall be shown forth the power of God and also his word, of which the Father, and the Son, and the Holy Ghost bear record — and all this shall stand as a testimony against the world at the last day. (*Ether* 5:2-4)

And my brother, Jacob, also has seen him as I have seen him; wherefore, I will send their words forth unto my children to prove unto them that my words are true. Wherefore, by the words of three, God hath said, I will establish my word. Nevertheless, God sendeth more witnesses, and he proveth all his words.   (2 *Nephi* 11:3)

IV

STATEMENT BY LUCY MACK SMITH

Mrs. Lucy Mack Smith relates some interesting circumstances in connection with the great vision of the Three Witnesses, and also gives the details of the time and place where the Eight Witnesses viewed the plates. This information is found in the new edition of Mrs. Smith's book, "History of the Prophet Joseph Smith," page 151-155.

As soon as the Book of Mormon was translated, Joseph dispatched a messenger to Mr. Smith, bearing intelligence of the completion of the work, and a request that Mr. Smith and myself should come immediately to Waterloo.

The same evening we conveyed this intelligence to Martin Harris, for we loved the man, although his weakness had cost us much trouble. Hearing this, he greatly rejoiced and determined to go straightway to Waterloo to congratulate Joseph upon his success. Accordingly, the next morning we all set off together and before sunset met Joseph and Oliver at Mr. Whitmer's.

The evening was spent in reading the manuscript, and it would be superfluous for me to say . . . that we rejoiced exceedingly. It then appeared to those of us who did not realize the magnitude of the work, as if the greatest difficulty was then surmounted; but Joseph better understood the nature of the dispensation of the Gospel which was committed unto him.

The next morning after attending to the usual services, namely, reading, singing and praying, Joseph arose from his knees, and approaching Martin Harris with a solemnity that thrills through my veins to this day, when it occurs to my recollection, said, "Martin Harris, you have got to humble yourself before God this day that you may obtain a forgiveness of your sins. If you do, it is the will of God that you should look upon the plates, in company with Oliver Cowdery and David Whitmer."

In a few minutes after this, Joseph, Martin, Oliver, and David, repaired to a grove a short distance from the house, where they commenced calling upon the Lord, and continued in earnest supplication until He permitted an angel to come down from His presence and declare to them that all which Joseph had testified of concerning the plates was true.

When they returned to the house it was between three and four o'clock p. m. Mrs. Whitmer, Mr. Smith and myself were sitting in a bedroom at the time. On coming in, Joseph threw himself down beside me and exclaimed, "Father, mother, you do not know how happy I am: The Lord has now caused the plates to be shown to three more besides myself. They have seen an angel, who has testified

[15]

to them, and they will have to bear witness to the truth of what I have said, for now they know for themselves that I do not go about to deceive the people, and I feel as if I was relieved of a burden which was almost too heavy for me to bear, and it rejoices my soul that I am not any longer to be entirely alone in the world." Upon this, Martin Harris came in. He seemed almost overcome with joy and testified boldly to what he had both seen and heard; and so did David and Oliver, adding that no tongue could express the joy in their hearts and the greatness of the things which they had both seen and heard. . . .

The following day, we returned, a cheerful, happy company. In a few days, we were followed by Joseph, Oliver and the Whitmers, who came to make us a visit and make some arrangements about getting the book printed. Soon after they came, all the male part of the company, with my husband, Samuel and Hyrum, retired to a place where the family were in the habit of offering up their secret devotions to God. They went to this place because it had been revealed to Joseph that the plates would be carried thither by one of the ancient Nephites. Here it was that those eight witnesses, whose names are recorded in the Book of Mormon, looked upon them and handled them. . . .

After these witnesses returned to the house, the angel again made his appearance to Joseph, at which time Joseph delivered up the plates into the angel's hands. That evening, we held a meeting in which all the witnesses bore testimony to the facts as stated above; and all of our family, even to Don Carlos, who was but fourteen years of age, testified of the truth of the Latter - day Dispensation — that it was then ushered in.

V

STATEMENT OF JOSEPH SMITH TO MR. WENTWORTH

The following clear, impressive statement was written or dictated by the Prophet Joseph Smith, probably in February 1842. It is found in the "History of the Church," vol. 4, page 535. Of this letter the Prophet Joseph Smith wrote: "At the request of Mr. John Wentworth, Editor and Proprietor of the Chicago Democrat, I have written the following sketch of the rise, progress, persecution and faith of the Latter-day Saints, of which I have the honor, under God, of being the founder. Mr. Wentworth says that he wishes to furnish Mr. Bastow, a friend of his, who is writing the history of New Hampshire, with this document. As Mr. Bastow has taken the proper steps to obtain correct information, all that I ask at his hands is that he publish the account entire, ungarnished and without misrepresentation."

For our purpose here we are publishing only that part of the letter which pertains to the coming forth of the Book of Mormon.

I WAS BORN in the town of Sharon, Windsor County, Vermont, on the 23rd of December, A.D. 1805. When ten years old, my parents removed to Palmyra, New York, where we resided about four years, and from thence we removed to the town of Manchester. My father was a farmer and taught me the art of husbandry. When about fourteen years of age, I began to reflect upon the importance of being prepared for a future state, and upon inquiring (about) the plan of salvation, I found that there was a great clash in religious sentiment; if I went to one society they referred me to one plan, and another to another; each one pointing to his own particular creed as the summum bonum of perfection. Considering that all could not be right, and that God could not be the author of so much confusion, I determined to investigate the subject more fully, believing that if God had a Church it would not split up into factions, and that if He taught one society to worship one way, and administer in one set of ordinances, He would not teach another, principles which were diametrically opposed.

Believing the word of God, I had confidence in the declaration of James — "If any of you lack wisdom, let him ask of God, that giveth to all men liberally, and upbraideth not; and it shall be given him." I retired to a secret place in a grove, and began to call upon the Lord; while fervently engaged in supplication, my mind was taken away from the objects with which I was surrounded, and I was enwrapped in a heavenly vision, and saw two glorious personages, who exactly resembled each other in features and likeness, surrounded with a brilliant light which eclipsed the sun at noon day. They told me that all religious denominations were believing in incorrect doctrines, and that none of them was acknowledged of God as His Church and kingdom, and I was expressly commanded "to go not after them," at the same time receiving a promise that the fulness of the Gospel should at some future time be made known unto me.

On the evening of the 21st of September, A.D. 1823, while I was praying unto God, and endeavoring to exercise faith in the precious promises of Scripture, of a sudden a light like that of day, only a far purer and more glorious appearance and brightness burst into the room, indeed the first sight was as though the house was filled with consuming fire; the appearance produced a shock that affected the whole body; in a moment a personage stood before me surrounded with a glory yet greater than that with which I was already surrounded. This messenger proclaimed himself to be an angel of God, sent to bring the joyful tidings that the covenant which God made with ancient Israel was at hand to be fulfilled, that the preparatory work for the second coming of the Messiah was speedily to commence; that the time was at hand for the Gospel in all its fulness to be preached in power, unto all nations, that a people might be prepared for the Millennial reign. I was informed that I was chosen to be an instrument in the hands of God to bring about some of His purposes in this glorious dispensation.

I was also informed concerning the aboriginal inhabitants of this country and shown who they were, and from whence they came; a brief sketch of their origin, progress, civilization, laws, governments, of their righteousness and iniquity, and the blessings of God being finally withdrawn from them as a people, was made known unto me; I was also told where were deposited some plates on which were engraven an abridgment of the records of the ancient Prophets that had existed on this continent. The angel appeared to me three times the same night and unfolded the same things. After having received many visits from the angels of God unfolding the majesty and glory of the events that should transpire in the last days, on the morning of the 22nd of September, A.D. 1827, the angel of the Lord delivered the records into my hands.

These records were engraven on plates which had the appearance of gold, each plate was six inches wide and eight inches long, and not quite so thick as common tin. They were filled with engravings, in Egyptian characters, and bound together in a volume as the leaves of a book, with three rings running through the whole. The volume was something near six inches in thickness, a part of which was sealed. The characters on the unsealed part were small, and beautifully engraved. The whole book exhibited many marks of antiquity in its construction, and much skill in the art of engraving. With the records was found a curious instrument, which the ancients called "Urim and Thummim," which consisted of two transparent stones set in the rim of a bow fastened to a breastplate. Through the medium of the Urim and Thummim I translated the record by the gift and power of God.

In this important and interesting book the history of ancient America is unfolded, from its first settlement by a colony that came from the Tower of Babel, at the confusion of languages to the beginning of the fifth century of the Christian Era. We are informed by these records that America in ancient times has been inhabited by two distinct races of people. The first were called Jaredites, and came directly from the Tower of Babel. The second race came directly from the city of Jerusalem, about six hundred years before Christ. They were principally Israelites, of the descendants of Joseph. The Jaredites were destroyed about the time that the Israelites came from Jerusalem, who succeeded them in the inheritance of the country. The principal nation of the second race fell in battle towards the close of the fourth century. The remnant are the Indians that now inhabit this country. This book also tells us that our Savior made His appearance upon this continent after His resurrection; that He planted the Gospel here in all its fulness, and richness, and power, and blessing; that they had Apostles, Prophets, Teachers and Evangelists; the same order, the same priesthood, the same ordinances, gifts, powers, and blessings, as were enjoyed on the eastern continent, that the people were cut off in consequence of their transgressions, that the last of their prophets who existed among them was commanded to write an abridgment of their prophecies, history, etc., and to hide it up in the earth, and that it should come forth and be united with the Bible for the accomplishment of the purposes of God in the last days. For a more particular account I would refer to the Book of Mormon, which can be purchased at Nauvoo, or from any of our Traveling Elders. . . .

VI

STATEMENT OF LUKE JOHNSON

The event described in the following statement is most remarkable. It is the only occasion in the history of the Church, as far as we have record, when the Eleven Witnesses of the Book of Mormon stood together, and with uplifted hands, bore testimony to the truth of the book. Also the statement of the Prophet Joseph Smith, on this occasion, that it was not expedient for him to relate more than was already known regarding the coming forth of the Book of Mormon, is most significant. The events related below took place at a conference of the Priesthood of the Church, held at Orange, Cuyahoga County, Ohio, October 25, 1831. We are indebted to Luke Johnson, an early convert to the Church, for this account.

At THIS CONFERENCE, the Eleven Witnesses of the Book of Mormon, with uplifted hands, bore solemn testimony to the truth of that book, as also did the Prophet Joseph. (*Millennial Star,* vol. 26, p. 835)

Brother Hyrum Smith said that he thought best that the information of the coming forth of the Book of Mormon be related by Joseph himself, to the Elders present, that all might know for themselves.

Brother Joseph Smith, Jun., said that it was not intended to tell the world all the particulars of the coming forth of the Book of Mormon; and also said that it was not expedient for him to relate these things. (*History of the Church,* vol. 1, p. 220)

VII

STATEMENT OF CONGRESSMAN DAVIS

During a visit which the Prophet Joseph Smith made to Washington, D.C., in the winter of 1839-40, when he endeavored to obtain redress from Congress and from the President of the United States for some of the wrongs done to the Saints in Missouri, he delivered a sermon on the doctrines of the Church, in one of the halls or churches of that city. Congressman Davis of New York City attended this meeting and reported the sermon to his wife. In his letter is found the following important sidelight as to the manner in which the Prophet translated the Book of Mormon.

THROUGHOUT HIS (Joseph Smith's) whole address he displayed strongly a spirit of charity and forbearance. The Mormon Bible, he said, was communicated to him direct from Heaven. If there was such a thing on earth as the author of it, then he (Smith) was the author; but the idea that he wished to impress was that he had penned it as dictated by God. (*History of the Church*, vol. 4, pp. 78-79)

VIII

STATEMENT BY
MRS. EMMA HALE SMITH BIDAMON

The following interesting record of a conversation between Joseph Smith, III, son of the Prophet Joseph Smith, and his mother, Mrs. Emma Hale Smith Bidamon, was published in October 1879, in the "Saints Advocate," the official publication of the Reorganized Church. Mrs. Bidamon died on the 30th of April, 1879, and this document was not published until six months after her death, consequently we have no knowledge that it was ever approved by her personally. After the death of the Prophet, in 1844, Mrs. Bidamon rejected completely the leadership of Brigham Young. She subsequently united with the Reorganized Church, which was founded by her son and a number of his friends, in 1860. We present the document as probable, historical information, from which the reader must draw his or her own conclusions. In the interview the questions were evidently asked by Joseph Smith, III, and answered by his mother.

FROM AN ARTICLE entitled "Last Testimony of Sister Emma," by Joseph Smith, III., Sister Emma was interviewed by her son, Joseph Smith, III.

Q. What of the truth of Mormonism?

A. I know Mormonism to be the truth, and believe the Church to have been established by divine direction. I have complete faith in it. In writing for your father, I frequently wrote day after day, often sitting at the table close to him, he sitting with his face buried in his hat, with the stone in it, and dictating hour after hour with nothing between us.[1]

Q. Had he not a book or manuscript from which to read or dictate to you?

A. He had neither manuscript nor book to read from.

Q. Could he not have had a book and you not know it?

A. If he had anything of the kind he could not have concealed it from me.

Q. Are you sure he had the plates at the time you were writing for him?

A. The plates often lay on the table without any attempt at concealment, wrapped in a small linen table cloth which I had given him to fold them in. I once felt of the plates, as they thus lay on the table, tracing their outline and shape. They seemed to be pliable like thick paper and would rustle with a metallic sound when the edges were moved by the thumb, as one does sometimes thumb the edges of a book.

Q. Where did father and Oliver Cowdery write?

A. Oliver Cowdery and your father wrote in the room where I was at work.

---

[1]The above statements do not agree with the statement made by the Prophet Joseph Smith. In the Wentworth letter the Prophet writes: "Through the Urim and Thummim I translated the record by the gift and power of God."

Q. Could not father have dictated the Book of Mormon to you, Oliver Cowdery and others who wrote for him, after having first written it or having first read it out of some book?

A. Joseph Smith (and for the first time she used his name direct, having usually used the words "your father" or "my husband") could neither write nor dictate a coherent and well-worded letter, let alone dictate a book like the Book of Mormon, and though I was an active participant in the scenes that transpired, was present during the translation of the plates, and had cognizance of things as they transpired, it is marvelous to me—a marvel and a wonder—as much as to anyone else.

Q. I should suppose that you would have uncovered the plates and examined them.

A. I did not attempt to handle the plates other than I have told you, nor uncover them to look at them. I was satisfied that it was the work of God and therefore did not feel it to be necessary to do so.

Major Bidamon here suggested, "Did Mr. Smith forbid your examining the plates?"

A. I do not think he did. I knew that he had them. I moved them from place to place on the table as it was necessary in doing my work.

Q. Mother, what is your belief about the authenticity of the Book of Mormon?

A. My belief is that the Book of Mormon is of divine authenticity — I have not the slightest doubt of it. I am satisfied that no man could have dictated the writing of the manuscripts unless he was inspired; for, when acting as his scribe, your father would dictate to me hour after hour; and when returning after meals, or interruptions, he would at once begin where he had left off, without either seeing the manuscript or having any portion of it read to him. This was a usual thing for him to do. It would have been improbable that a learned man could do this, and for one so ignorant and unlearned as he was, it was simply impossible. . . .

Part Two

★ ★ ★ ★

OLIVER COWDERY

I

SKETCH OF THE LIFE OF
OLIVER COWDERY

Following is a brief sketch of the life of Oliver Cowdery, one of the witnesses of the Book of Mormon, taken principally from the account written by Andrew Jenson, and found in his "L.D.S. Biographical Encyclopedia," vol. 1, page 246.

O LIVER COWDERY, the "second Elder of the Church," and one of the Three Witnesses of the Book of Mormon, was born in the town of Wells, Rutland County, Vermont, on October 3rd, 1806. His parents were farming people of the neighborhood. When Oliver was three years of age, he removed with his father's family to Poultney, Vermont, and here he grew up, helping to assist his father on the farm, until 1825 when the family moved again — this time to the western part of the state of New York.

For a time after his arrival in New York, Oliver was engaged as a clerk in a store, but in the winter of 1828 and 1829 he accepted the position of teacher in a small rural school in Manchester township. Among the families who sent children to his school was that of Joseph Smith, Sr., a farmer of the neighborhood.

It was the custom of that day for the village schoolteacher to board with the families who sent children to his school. Oliver Cowdery thus became acquainted with the members of the Smith family, and for a time he made his residence with them. From them, in their quiet family circle, he heard the wonderful story of the visit of the angel Moroni to their son Joseph; the story of the finding of the Sacred Record, and of the efforts of the young Prophet to translate the same so that it might be given to the world.

Oliver Cowdery became deeply interested and determined to visit Joseph, who, at the time, made his home in Harmony, Pennsylvania.

It was on April 5, 1829, that Oliver arrived in Harmony, having accompanied Joseph's younger brother Samuel on the journey. Two days later, Oliver began to write for Joseph while the latter translated the ancient characters written upon the plates.

As the interesting work progressed, Oliver became exceedingly anxious to have the gift of translation conferred upon himself. Joseph inquired of the Lord and received two enlightening revelations in regard to the matter, and pertaining to the duties of both himself and Oliver (See sections 8 and 9 of the Doctrine and Covenants).

After about five weeks of continuous labor, Joseph and Oliver came upon certain passages in the plates which pertained to the subject of baptism. Realizing that they themselves had not been baptized, they decided to seek information from the Lord in prayer concerning this important subject. It was on May 15, 1829, that they knelt in prayer, on the banks of the Susquehanna River, near Joseph's home.

While thus engaged, a messenger from heaven descended in a cloud of light and, laying his hands upon them he ordained them, saying: "Upon you my fellow servants, in the name of Messiah I confer the Priesthood of Aaron, which holds the keys of the ministering of angels, and of the gospel of repentance, and of baptism by immersion for the remission of sins; and this shall never be taken again from the earth, until the sons of Levi do offer again an offering unto the Lord in righteousness."

The Heavenly Messenger said that the Aaronic Priesthood did not have power to confer the Holy Ghost by the laying on of hands. He told them that his name was John. The same that is called John the Baptist in the New Testament, and that he acted under the direction of Peter, James and John, who held the keys of the Priesthood of Melchizedek, which Priesthood he said would in due time be conferred upon them, when Joseph should be the first Elder of the Church and Oliver the second Elder. The Heavenly Messenger also instructed them to baptize each other, and directed that Joseph should baptize Oliver, and that Oliver should baptize Joseph. The brethren complied immediately with this request and the ordinance was performed in the nearby Susquehanna River. Joseph then laid his hands on Oliver and ordained him to the Aaronic Priesthood. Oliver followed with the same procedure and ordained Joseph to the same Priesthood.

The exact date when the Melchizedek Priesthood was conferred by Peter, James and John is not known, but historians are generally agreed that this important event took place shortly after the bestowal of the Aaronic Priesthood.

Due to persecution which developed in the neighborhood of Harmony, Joseph felt that he and Oliver would be forced to move away. Oliver thereupon wrote to David Whitmer of Fayette township, New York, with the request that he and Joseph be permitted to finish their important work at his father's home. Arrangements were satisfactorily concluded and about the first of June, 1829, David Whitmer arrived at Harmony with a two-horse wagon to convey Joseph, Emma, Oliver and the Sacred Record to Fayette.

Arriving at the Whitmer home, the work of translation was immediately resumed, and in about four weeks time the great and important work was concluded. From David Whitmer we have the information that the translation was finished "in the latter part of June 1829."

The vision of the Three Witnesses, of which

Oliver Cowdery was permitted to be a member, occurred a few days after the translation was completed, in a grove near the Whitmer home.

After arrangements were made by Joseph Smith and Martin Harris to have the manuscript of the Book of Mormon published, Oliver Cowdery was assigned the task of making a printer's copy and looking after the details during publication. This work was performed in a satisfactory manner.

On April 6, 1830, the Church was organized in Fayette, New York, and Oliver Cowdery was one of the six original members. It was on that occasion that he was ordained by Joseph Smith to be the second Elder of the Church. On April 11th Oliver preached the first public discourse given by any member of the Church. Thereafter he was very active as a missionary of the Church during the entire summer and fall of 1830, assisting the Prophet in every way possible.

In October 1830, Oliver Cowdery, Parley P. Pratt, Peter Whitmer, Jr., and Ziba Peterson were called by revelation to undertake a mission to the Lamanites residing on the western border of the United States.

Experiencing great hardships, and traveling mostly on foot, the four brethren reached Independence, Missouri, early in the year 1831. Here they began their labors and here Oliver Cowdery and two of his companions remained until the arrival of the Prophet Joseph and several companions in July following, when Jackson County was designated by revelation as the gathering place of the Saints and a site was selected and dedicated on which a temple was to be built.

In the month of August, Oliver Cowdery returned to Kirtland with the Prophet and several companions, and the day following his arrival he was ordained a High Priest by Sidney Rigdon.

In November 1831, Oliver Cowdery and John Whitmer were sent to Independence with the revelations, which were to be published there by William W. Phelps. Shortly after Oliver's arrival, on January 22, 1832, he was married to Elizabeth Ann Whitmer. The marriage took place on Elizabeth's seventeenth birthday; Oliver at the time was twenty-five years of age.

During the Prophet's second visit to Missouri in the summer of 1832, Oliver was appointed one of the High Priests to preside over the Saints in the gathering place.

When the serious trouble between the old settlers of Jackson County and the Saints broke out in July 1833, Oliver was sent as a messenger to the First Presidency at Kirtland to inform them of the disaster. Following his arrival he was asked to take charge of a publication known as the *Evening and Morning Star.* At the dedication of the press, which was held on December 18, 1833, Oliver Cowdery was present, and the same day the Prophet recorded the following blessing in his history: "Blessed of the Lord is Brother

Oliver; nevertheless there are two evils in him that he must need forsake, or he cannot altogether forsake the buffetings of the adversary. If he forsake these evils he shall be forgiven, and he shall be made like unto the bow which the Lord hath set in the heavens; he shall be a sign and an ensign to the nations. Behold, he is blessed of the Lord for his constancy and steadfastness in the work of the Lord; wherefore he shall be blessed in his generation, and they shall never be cut off, and he shall be helped out of many troubles; and if he keeps the commandments and hearkens unto the counsel of the Lord, his rest shall be glorious."

At the organization of the first High Council of the Church in Kirtland, on February 17, 1834, Oliver Cowdery was selected to be a member. When the Prophet, with Zion's Camp, started for Missouri in May following, Sidney Rigdon and Oliver were left in charge of the Church at Kirtland.

After the Prophet's return, on the evening of November 29, 1834, he and Oliver Cowdery united in prayer, and made a covenant that of the means that came to them they would give "a tenth" to be bestowed upon the poor of the Church, "or as he shall command." This was the first introduction of the tithing principle among the Latter-day Saints.

In February, 1835, the Three Witnesses of the Book of Mormon, Oliver Cowdery, David Whitmer and Martin Harris, chose twelve men from the Elders of the Church, to be members of the Quorum of

Twelve Apostles. In blessing them and giving them instructions, Oliver Cowdery took a prominent part. He was also one of the trustees of the school in Kirtland, where he studied Hebrew, in connection with the Prophet and other Elders. On September 14, 1835, he was appointed to act as Church Recorder. He had previously held the same office from April 1830 to June 1831.

Elder Cowdery was present at the dedication of the Kirtland Temple in March 1836, and took a prominent part in the proceedings. On April 3, 1836, he was with the Prophet in the Kirtland Temple when they beheld the great vision of Moses, Elias, and Elijah; and the Savior of mankind appeared before them. In September of the following year, 1837, Oliver Cowdery was appointed to be the assistant-counselor to the President of the Church.

Despite his great privileges and experiences, Oliver Cowdery practically rejected the leadership of the Prophet during the latter part of 1837 and early in 1838. He opposed several important measures which Joseph Smith advocated.

As a result, the High Council at Far West, Missouri, where Oliver was residing at the time, took action against him on April 11, 1838, and the following day excommunicated him from the Church.

For a period of ten years Oliver Cowdery was not connected with the organization he had so materially assisted in founding. During the years 1838 to 1848 he practiced law in Ohio and Wisconsin.

In October 1848, Oliver Cowdery, with his wife and daughter, arrived at Council Bluffs, Iowa, the gathering place of the Saints who were preparing to make the long journey across the plains to Utah. Here he requested of Orson Hyde, who was presiding over that branch at the time, the privilege of again being baptized into the Church. At a special conference of the members held on October 21st, the request was granted and shortly afterwards Oliver Cowdery was baptized by Orson Hyde.

In the spring of 1849, Oliver Cowdery expressed the desire to visit with his wife's family in Richmond, Missouri, before undertaking the long journey across the plains. Accordingly, the trip was made to that place, and there, as a guest of his father-in-law, Peter Whitmer, in whose home near Waterloo, New York, the church had been organized, he spent several pleasant months. As the result of a severe cold, contracted sometime during 1849, he became infected with the dreaded disease known then as "consumption," which brought about his death on March 3, 1850. Oliver Cowdery, at the time, was a few months past his 43rd birthday. Of his death, David Whitmer, who was present, relates:

"Oliver died the happiest man I ever saw. After shaking hands with the family and kissing his wife and daughter, he said: 'Now I lay me down for the last time: I am going to my Savior'; and he died immediately with a smile on his face."

II

ACCOUNT BY JUDGE C. M. NIELSEN

---

*The following interesting event in the life of Oliver
Cowdery was related by Judge C. M. Nielsen of Salt Lake
City, and was published in the "Liahona" on August 30,
1910. It gives conclusive proof that Oliver Cowdery was
faithful to his testimony of the divinity of the Book of Mormon, and that he fearlessly proclaimed that testimony during the years that he was out of the Church, from 1838
to 1848.*

IN THE YEAR 1884 I was traveling as a missionary
in Minnesota. I had most of the eastern part of
the state to myself. I was without purse or scrip and
one night slept in a haystack. Next day I came to
a city and wandered up and down the streets. I had
no money, no friends and didn't know where to go.
I passed a large store called the Emporium, something like our Z.C.M.I. I was attracted by it, but
didn't know why. There were about 25 teams hitched
near the place, owned by farmers in town on business. Something told me to "Go over and see a certain man." The street was full of people and I wondered which man. Then one man seemed to me as
big as three ordinary men. The spirit whispered:
"Go over and speak to him!" I hesitated to approach

this entire stranger, but the same voice came to me a second and a third time. Then I went.

He was a prosperous-looking farmer with a fine two-seated buggy, which he was ready to enter, and was a prominent man, I afterwards learned. Not knowing what else to say, I said: "How far are you going?" "Home; where are you going?" "I have no certain place, I am from Utah." "You are not a Mormon, are you?" he asked, anxiously. "Yes." "Then God bless you!" he replied, reaching out his arms and dropping the lines. "Get into this buggy as fast as you can. When we get home my wife will rejoice as I rejoice now; I will then explain all. But you are not one of these make-believers are you?" "No, I'm a real live Mormon from Utah."

Reaching the home, he called, "Mother, here's a real live Mormon Elder." I'm afraid I didn't look very fine, as I had slept in a haystack the previous night. They took me by the hand and led me into the house. I was very hungry and begged for something to eat. After my hunger was satisfied, they called in their sons and daughters and we sat around the table. My new-found friend then said:

"Now, young man, you thought it strange how I acted when you spoke to me. When I get through you will realize the importance of your coming to us. When I was 21 years of age, I was working my father's farm in Michigan. I had worked hard on the farm that summer and decided to take a day off,

[43]

so went to the city. Near the courthouse I saw a great many people assembling and others walking that way, so I went over to see what was up. There was a jam in the courtroom, but being young and strong, I pushed my way close up to the center, where I found the prosecuting attorney addressing the court and jury in a murder trial. The prosecuting attorney was Oliver Cowdery, and he was giving his opening address in behalf of the state. (After he was excommunicated from the Church, Oliver Cowdery studied law, practicing in Ohio, Wisconsin and then Michigan, where he was elected prosecuting attorney.) After Cowdery sat down the attorney representing the prisoner arose and with taunting sarcasm said: 'May it plaese the court and gentlemen of the jury, I see one Oliver Cowdery is going to reply to my argument. I wish he would tell us something about that golden Bible that Joe Smith dug out of the hill; something about the great fraud he perpetrated upon the American people whereby he gained thousands of dollars. Now he seems to know so much about this poor prisoner, I wonder if he has forgotten all about Joe Smith and his connection with him.' The speaker all the while sneering and pointing his finger in scorn at Cowdery in the hope of making him ridiculous before the court and jury.

"Everybody present began to wonder if they had been guilty of making such a mistake as choosing a Mormon for prosecuting attorney. Even the judge on the bench began looking with suspicion and distrust at the prosecuting attorney. The prisoner and his attorney became elated at the effect of the speech. People began asking, 'Is he a Mormon?' Everybody wondered what Cowdery would say against such foul charges.

"Finally Oliver Cowdery arose, calm as a summer morning. I was within three feet of him. There was no hesitation, no fear, no anger in his voice, as he said: 'May it please the court, and gentlemen of the jury, my brother attorney on the other side has charged me with connection with Joseph Smith and the golden Bible. The responsibility has been placed upon me, and I cannot escape reply. Before God and man I dare not deny what I have said, and what my testimony contains as written and printed on the front page of the Book of Mormon. May it please your honor and gentlemen of the jury, this I say, I saw the angel and heard his voice—how can I deny it? It happened in the daytime when the sun was shining bright in the firmament; not in the night when I was asleep. That glorious messenger from heaven, dressed in white, standing above the ground, in a glory I have never seen anything to compare with—the sun insignificant in comparison—and this personage told us if we denied that testimony there is no forgiveness in this life nor in the world to come. Now how can I deny it—I dare not; I will not!'"

The man who related this to me was a prominent man in that state; he was a rich man, a man who has held offices of trust from the people — a man of respect, one when you look into his face you will not doubt. To strengthen his statement this man, who knew nothing of "Mormon" history, said Oliver Cowdery mentioned something he wanted me to explain—that the angel took back a part that was not translated. We know this and that part of the golden plates then withheld will be revealed at some future time.

"Since I heard Oliver Cowdery speak," continued my host, "I have not had peace for these many years. I want to know more about your people. I felt when I listened to Oliver Cowdery talking in the courtroom he was more than an ordinary man. If you can show us that you have what Oliver Cowdery testified to, we shall all be glad to receive it." (*Liahona*, August 30, 1910)

III

OLIVER COWDERY'S RETURN TO
THE CHURCH

The return of Oliver Cowdery to the Church took place during the early part of October 1848, when he arrived at the small settlement of Kanesville, Iowa, accompanied by his wife and daughter. He was received in a friendly manner by the brethren who resided there and at a conference of the Church held at Kanesville on October 21st, he was invited to speak. His remarks were preserved for us by Bishop Reuben Miller, who was present at the meeting, and were later published in the "Millennial Star," vol. 21, pp. 544-546.

FOLLOWING is a verbatim report: "Friends and Brethren—My name is Cowdery, Oliver Cowdery. In the early history of this Church I stood identified with her, and was one in her councils. True it is that the gifts and callings of God are without repentance. Not because I was better than the rest of mankind was I called; but, to fulfill the purposes of God, He called me to a high and holy calling.

"I wrote, with my own pen, the entire Book of Mormon (save a few pages) as it fell from the lips of the Prophet Joseph Smith, as he translated it by the gift and power of God, by the means of the Urim and Thummim, or, as it is called by that book, 'holy interpreters.' I beheld with my eyes and handled with my hands the gold plates from which it was transcribed. I also saw with my eyes and handled with my hands the 'holy interpreters.' That book is true. Sidney Rigdon did not write it; Mr. Spaulding did not write it; I wrote it myself as it fell from the lips of the Prophet. It contains the Everlasting Gospel, and came forth to the children of men in fulfillment of the revelations of John, where he says he saw an angel come with the Everlasting Gospel to preach to every nation, kindred, tongue and people. It contains the principles of salvation; and if you, my hearers, will walk by its light and obey its precepts, you will be saved with an everlasting salvation in the kingdom of God on high. Brother Hyde has just said that it is very important that we keep and walk in the true channel, in order to avoid the sand-bars. This is true. The channel is here. The holy Priesthood is here.

"I was present with Joseph when an holy angel from God came down from heaven and conferred on us, or restored, the lesser or Aaronic Priesthood, and said to us, at the same time, that it should remain upon the earth while the earth stands.

"I was also present with Joseph when the higher or Melchizedek Priesthood was conferred by holy angels from on high. This Priesthood we then conferred on each other, by the will and commandment of God. This Priesthood, as was then declared, is

[48]

also to remain upon the earth until the last remnant of time. This holy Priesthood, or authority, we then conferred upon many and is just as good and valid as though God had done it in person.

"I laid my hands upon that man—yes, I laid my right hand upon his head (pointing to Brother Hyde), and I conferred upon him this Priesthood, and he holds that Priesthood now. He was also called through me, by the prayer of faith, an Apostle of the Lord Jesus Christ."

In the early part of November following, Elder Hyde called a High Council meeting in the log Tabernacle to consider the case of Oliver Cowdery; having been cut off by the voice of a High Council, it was thought that, if he was restored, he should be restored by the voice of a similar body. Before this body Brother Cowdery said:

"Brethren, for a number of years I have been separated from you. I now desire to come back. I wish to come humbly and to be one in your midst. I seek no station; I only wish to be identified with you. I am out of the Church. I am not a member of the Church, but I wish to become a member of it. I wish to come in at the door. I know the door. I have not come here to seek precedence. I come humbly and throw myself upon the decisions of this body, knowing as I do that its decisions are right and should be obeyed."

Brother George W. Harris, President of the Council, moved that Brother Cowdery be received. Considerable discussion took place in relation to a certain letter which, it was alleged, Brother Cowdery had written to David Whitmer. Brother Cowdery again rose and said:

"If there be any person that has aught against me, let him declare it. My coming back and humbly asking to become a member, through the door, covers the whole ground. I acknowledge this authority."

Brother Hyde moved that Brother Oliver Cowdery be received into the Church by baptism and that all old things be dropped and forgotten, which was seconded and carried unanimously. Soon afterwards he was re-baptized.

IV

STATEMENT OF EDWARD STEVENSON

In an article published in the "Millennial Star," under date of July 5, 1886, Elder Edward Stevenson paid the following tribute to Oliver Cowdery.

I HAVE OFTEN heard him bear a faithful testimony to the restoration of the Gospel by the visitation of an angel, in whose presence he stood in company with the Prophet Joseph Smith and David Whitmer. He testified that he beheld the plates, the leaves being turned over by the angel, whose voice he heard, and that they were commanded as witnesses to bear a faithful testimony to the world of the vision that they were favored to behold, and that the translation from the plates of the Book of Mormon was accepted of the Lord, and that it should go forth to the world, and no power on earth should stop its progress. Although for a time Oliver Cowdery absented himself from the body of the Church, I never have known a time when he faltered or was recreant to the trust so sacredly entrusted to him by an angel from heaven.

LAST TESTIMONY OF OLIVER COWDERY

Further testimony regarding Oliver Cowdery was published in the "Improvement Era," vol. 2, pp. 90-96, in an article by Samuel W. Richards. Oliver Cowdery visited with Samuel W. Richards while on his way to Missouri in 1849.

IN 1848, a yearning which Oliver Cowdery had for the society of those with whom he had once been so familiar, caused him to visit Kanesville, Iowa, where Orson Hyde, then president of the Twelve Apostles, was residing, and make application for a reunion with the Church, which was granted by his being baptized and duly admitted into the Church by Elder Hyde officiating.

Soon after this, with the view of joining the Saints in Salt Lake valley the next season, he, with his wife, desired first to visit her brother, David Whitmer, then living in Richmond, Missouri. For this purpose, in the month of January (1949), they started on the journey by team, but were overtaken by a severe snowstorm which compelled them to seek shelter, which they obtained with the writer of this article, then temporarily residing in the upper part of that state. Here they found it necessary to remain some length of time on account of the great amount of snow which had fallen, completely blockading the road, and for a time preventing travel by teams.

This detention of nearly two weeks time was extremely interesting, and made very enjoyable to both parties participating in the social and intellectual feast so unexpectedly provided.

I had but the fall before returned from my first mission to the British Isles, and was in the spirit of inquiry as to all matters of early history and experiences in the Church, and soon found there was no reserve on the part of Oliver in answering my many questions. In doing so his mind seemed as fresh in the recollection of events, which occurred more than a score of years before, as though they were but of yesterday.

Upon carefully inquiring as to his long absence from the body of the Church, he stated that he had never met the Prophet Joseph, after his expulsion from the Church, while he lived, apparently feeling that the Prophet could, with equal propriety, inquire after him, as for him to visit the Prophet, and as his pride would seemingly not allow him to become a suppliant without that, it was never made; while he felt quite sure that had he ever met the Prophet there would have been no difficulty in effecting a reconciliation, as a feeling of jealousy towards him, on the part of his accusers, had entered largely into their purpose of having him removed, which he thought Joseph must have discovered after going to Missouri.

In what had now transpired with him he felt to acknowledge the hand of God, in that he had been preserved; for if he had been with the Church he would have undoubtedly been with Joseph in his days of trial and shared a like fate with him; but being spared, he now desired to go to the nations and bear a testimony of this work which no other living man could bear; and he decided to go to the Presidency of the Church and offer his services for that purpose.

This indeed seemed to be his only ambition, and he was now going to visit his wife's brother, David Whitmer, and prepare to go to the mountains and join the body of the Church the following summer and unite with them. For some cause this was not permitted, and he died in Missouri among relatives before realizing the intent and purpose he had cherished of again testifying of the great work and dispensation, which he had been instrumental, with the Prophet, in opening up to the world.

To hear him describe, in his pleasant but earnest manner, the personality of those heavenly messengers, with whom he and the Prophet had so freely held converse, was enchanting to my soul. Their heavenly appearance, clothed in robes of purity; the influence of their presence, so lovely and serene; their eyes, that seemed to penetrate to the very depths of the soul, together with the color of the eyes that gazed upon them, were all so beautifully related as to almost make one feel that they were then present. . . .

Before taking his departure he wrote and left with the writer of this, the following statement, which we believe to be his last living testimony, though oft repeated, of the wonderful manifestations which brought the authority of God to men on the earth:

"While darkness covered the earth and gross darkness the people; long after the authority to administer in holy things had been taken away, the Lord opened the heavens and sent forth His word for the salvation of Israel. In fulfillment of the sacred scriptures, the everlasting gospel was proclaimed by the mighty angel (Moroni) who, clothed with the authority of his mission, gave glory to God in the highest. This gospel is the 'stone taken from the mountain without hands.' John the Baptist, holding the keys of the Aaronic Priesthood; Peter, James and John, holding the keys of the Melchizedek Priesthood, have also ministered for those who shall be heirs of salvation, and with these administrations, ordained men to the same Priesthoods. These Priesthoods, with their authority, are now, and must continue to be, in the body of the Church of Jesus Christ of Latter-day Saints. Blessed is the Elder who has received the same, and thrice blessed and holy is he who shall endure to the end.

"Accept assurances, dear brother, of the unfeigned prayer of him who, in connection with Joseph the Seer, was blessed with the above minis-

[55]

trations, and who earnestly and devoutly hopes to meet you in the celestial glory.

"OLIVER COWDERY.

"To Samuel W. Richards, January 13, 1849."

VI

STATEMENTS OF LUCY P. YOUNG
AND PHINEAS H. YOUNG

In Andrew Jenson's sketch of the life of Oliver Cowdery, published in vol. 1, pp. 246-251, of the "L.D.S. Biographical Encyclopedia," there are the following interesting statements by Lucy P. Young and Phineas H. Young.

OLIVER COWDERY'S HALF-SISTER, Lucy P. Young, widow of Phineas H. Young, relates the circumstances of Oliver's death: Just before breathing his last, he asked his attendants to raise him up in bed that he might talk to the family and his friends who were present. He then told them to live according to the teachings contained in the Book of Mormon, and promised them if they would do this that they would meet him in heaven. He then said, "Lay me down and let me fall asleep." A few moments later he died, without a struggle.

Elder Phineas H. Young, who was present at the death of Oliver Cowdery, at Richmond, Missouri, March 3, 1850, says, "His last moments were spent in bearing testimony of the truth of the Gospel revealed through Joseph Smith, and the power of the holy Priesthood which he had received through his administrations."

[57]

Part Three

* * *

DAVID WHITMER

I

SKETCH OF THE LIFE OF
DAVID WHITMER

We now come to the second witness of the Book of Mormon, David Whitmer, and reproduce below the account of his life adapted from the sketch written by Andrew Jenson and found in his "Biographical Encyclopedia," vol. 1, pages 203 to 212, inclusive.

DAVID WHITMER was born at a small trading post near Harrisburg, Pennsylvania, on January 7, 1805. While yet an infant, his father, who had served his country through the Revolutionary War, moved with his family to western New York, and settled on a farm in Seneca County, two miles from Waterloo, seven from Geneva, and twenty-five miles from Palmyra, where David lived until 1831.

The father, Peter Whitmer, was a hard-working, God-fearing man, a strict Presbyterian who brought his children up with rigid sectarian discipline. Besides two daughters, Catherine, who married Hiram Page, and Elizabeth, who married Oliver Cowdery, there were five sons—Peter, Jacob, John, David and Christian.

David was working on his father's farm in 1828, when he made a business trip to Palmyra. There he learned from Oliver Cowdery, whom it appears he had known for some time, the rumors which were going about the countryside that Joseph Smith, Jr., had been directed in heavenly vision to a hill in the neighborhood, and there he had been given some "Gold plates," which contained a record of ancient peoples who once inhabited this continent. Oliver Cowdery told David Whitmer that he intended to investigate the matter, and a short time later he left for Harmony, Pennsylvania, where Joseph Smith, Jr., resided. From there he wrote David that he had every evidence to believe that Joseph had the plates. Some weeks later David received another letter from Oliver to the effect that he and Joseph feared persecution from the residents of Harmony and requested David to come and get them and take them to his father's house. David complied with this request and it was at his father's home, during the latter part of June, 1829, that the translation was finished. "I, as well as all of my father's family, Joseph's wife, Oliver Cowdery and Martin Harris were present during the translation," wrote David in later years.

The great vision of the Three Witnesses occurred a few days after the translation of the Book of Mormon was completed.

The organization of the Church took place at the Peter Whitmer home on April 6, 1830, and David Whitmer was one of the first six named members. It was also some time during the year 1830 that

David was married to Julia A. Jolly, a young woman in the neighborhood of the Whitmer family.

In the summer of 1831, David Whitmer, with most of the members of his father's family, migrated to the state of Ohio, which had become the headquarters of the Church. At a conference held at Orange, Ohio, on October 25, 1831, he was ordained a High Priest by Oliver Cowdery.

In the spring of 1832, David Whitmer, with his own and with members of his father's family, migrated again to the west and settled near Independence, in Jackson County, Missouri. Here they hoped to remain and become permanently identified with the up-building of the Church, but in 1833 they, with all the Saints in the county, were expelled from their farms and peaceful habitations by a vicious mob of old settlers who feared that the Mormons would gain political control of the county and garner all the offices.

David, with many of the Saints, crossed the Missouri River and settled in Clay County, and there in the summer of 1834 he was made president of the High Council, organized by the Prophet Joseph Smith.

During the summer of 1837 David Whitmer visited the headquarters of the Church in Kirtland, and while there he showed signs of disaffection, and finally completely rejected the leadership of the Prophet. On his return to Missouri he was excommunicated from the Church by the High Council at Far West, on April 13, 1838. Subsequently he moved to Richmond, Ray County, and there spent the balance of his life on a farm, well respected by his neighbors as an honest and reliable citizen. On every occasion that presented itself he affirmed his testimony, as printed in the Book of Mormon, concerning the great vision of the Three Witnesses. His death occurred on January 25, 1888.

II

INTERVIEW BETWEEN DAVID WHITMER,
ORSON PRATT AND JOSEPH F. SMITH

---

*The following interviews, between David Whitmer,
Orson Pratt and Joseph F. Smith, took place at Richmond,
Missouri, on the 7th and 8th of September, 1878. Elders
Pratt and Smith had gone east from Salt Lake City to visit
the historical sites of the Church. On their way they stop-
ped off at Richmond, Missouri, to interview David Whit-
mer, the last surviving witness of the Book of Mormon.
Joseph F. Smith committed to writing the interview which
is printed below, and which is to be found in the "Millennial
Star," vol. 40, pp. 771-774.*

AT RICHMOND we put up at the Shaw House (before the cyclone a three-story brick building,
but has been restored since the tempest, only two
stories), now kept by Mr. Warren Ewing, son-in-law
to the original proprietor, Mr. S. Shaw, once a
freighter to Utah, now dead. On Saturday morning,
September 7th, we met Mr. David Whitmer, the last
remaining one of the three witnesses to the Book of
Mormon. He is a good-sized man, 73 years of age
last January, and well-preserved (he was born January 7, 1805). He is close-shaven, his hair perfectly
white and rather thin; he has a large head and a

very pleasant, manly countenance that one would readily perceive to be an index to a conscientious, honest heart. He seemed wonderfully pleased, as well as surprised, at seeing Elder Orson Pratt. Said he would not have known him—he had grown so fat and stout; he remembered him as a slender, bashful, timid boy. After a few moments conversation he excused himself, saying he would return again to see us. This meeting was in the barroom of the hotel. When he called again he was in company with Col. Childs, a middle-aged man, and a resident of the place. By invitation we accompanied them to Mr. Whitmer's office, where we were introduced to Mr. David J. Whitmer (eldest son of David), Mr. Geo. Schweich (grandson of the old gentleman), Mr. John C. Whitmer (son of Jacob Whitmer), Col. James W. Black, of Richmond, and several others. A couple of hours were very pleasantly passed in conversation, principally on Utah matters, when we parted for dinner, agreeing to meet Mr. Whitmer again at his office at 4:30 p.m.

Agreeable to appointment, we met Mr. Whitmer and his friends at his office, but as the place was too public for private conversation and as it seemed impossible to obtain a private personal interview with David Whitmer, by himself, we invited him and such of his friends as he saw proper to fetch along, to our room in the hotel. Mr. Whitmer apologized for not inviting us to his house, as it was "wash day," and he and his wife were "worn out" with the extra labor,

[66]

exposure, etc., etc., consequent on rebuilding since the cyclone. He accepted our invitation to our room and brought with him James R. B. Vancleave, a fine-looking, intelligent, young newspaper man of Chicago, who is paying his addresses to Miss Josephine Schweich (granddaughter of David Whitmer), George Schweich (grandson), John C. Whitmer (son of Jacob), W. W. Warner, and another person whose name we did not learn. In the presence of these, the following, in substance, as noticed in Brother Joseph F. Smith's journal, is the account of the interview.

Elder O. Pratt to D. Whitmer. Can you tell the date of the bestowal of the Apostleship upon Joseph, by Peter, James and John?

D. W. I do not know, Joseph never told me. I can only tell you what I know, for I will not testify to anything I do not know.

J. F. S. to D. W. Did Oliver Cowdery die here in Richmond?

D. W. Yes, he lived here, I think, about one year before his death. He died in my father's house, right here, in March, 1850. Phineas Young was here at the time.

Elder O. P. Do you remember what time you saw the plates?

D. W. It was in June, 1829 — the latter part of the month, and the eight witnesses saw them, I think, the next day or the day after (i.e. one or two days after). Joseph showed them the plates himself, but the angel showed us (the three witnesses) the plates, as I suppose to fulfill the words of the book itself. Martin Harris was not with us at this time; he obtained a view of them afterwards (the same day). Joseph, Oliver and myself were together when I saw them. We not only saw the plates of the Book of Mormon but also the brass plates, the plates of the Book of Ether, the plates containing the records of the wickedness and secret combinations of the people of the world down to the time of their being engraved, and many other plates. The fact is, it was just as though Joseph, Oliver and I were sitting just here on a log, when we were overshadowed by a light. It was not like the light of the sun nor like that of a fire, but more glorious and beautiful. It extended away round us, I cannot tell how far, but in the midst of this light about as far off as he sits (pointing to John C. Whitmer, sitting a few feet from him), there appeared as it were, a table with many records or plates upon it, besides the plates of the Book of Mormon, also the Sword of Laban, the Directors — i.e., the ball which Lehi had — and the Interpreters. I saw them just as plain as I see this bed (striking the bed beside him with his hand), and I heard the voice of the Lord, as distinctly as I ever heard anything in my life, declaring that the records of the plates of the Book of Mormon were translated by the gift and power of God.

Elder O. P. Did you see the angel at this time?

D. W. Yes; he stood before us. Our testimony as recorded in the Book of Mormon is strictly and absolutely true, just as it is there written. Before I knew Joseph, I had heard about him and the plates from persons who declared they knew he had them, and swore they would get them from him. When Oliver Cowdery went to Pennsylvania, he promised to write me what he should learn about these matters, which he did. He wrote me that Joseph had told him his (Oliver's) secret thoughts, and all he had meditated about going to see him, which no man on earth knew, as he supposed, but himself, and so he stopped to write for Joseph.

Soon after this, Joseph sent for me (D. W.) to come to Harmony to get him and Oliver and bring them to my father's house. I did not know what to do, I was pressed with my work. I had some 20 acres to plow, so I concluded I would finish plowing and then go. I got up one morning to go to work as usual and, on going to the field, found between five and seven acres of my ground had been plowed during the night.

I don't know who did it; but it was done just as I would have done it myself, and the plow was left standing in the furrow.

This enabled me to start sooner. When I arrived at Harmony, Joseph and Oliver were coming toward me, and met me some distance from the house. Oliver told me that Joseph had informed him when I started from home, where I had stopped the first night, how I read the sign at the tavern, where I stopped the next night, etc., and that I would be there that day before dinner, and this was why they had come out to meet me; all of which was exactly as Joseph had told Oliver, at which I was greatly astonished. When I was returning to Fayette, with Joseph and Oliver, all of us riding in the wagon, Oliver and I on an old-fashioned, wooden, spring seat and Joseph behind us; while traveling along in a clear open place, a very pleasant, nice-looking old man suddenly appeared by the side of our wagon and saluted us with, "Good morning, it is very warm," at the same time wiping his face or forehead with his hand. We returned the salutation, and, by a sign from Joseph, I invited him to ride if he was going our way. But he said very pleasantly, "No, I am going to Cumorah." This name was something new to me, I did not know what Cumorah meant. We all gazed at him and at each other, and as I looked around inquiringly of Joseph, the old man instantly disappeared, so that I did not see him again.

J. F. S. Did you notice his appearance?

D. W. I should think I did. He was, I should think, about 5 feet 8 or 9 inches tall and heavy set, about such a man as James Vancleave there, but heavier; his face was as large, he was dressed in a suit of brown woolen clothes, his hair and beard were white, like Brother Pratt's, but his beard was not so heavy. I also remember that he had on his back a sort of knapsack with something in, shaped like a book. It was the messenger who had the plates, who had taken them from Joseph just prior to our starting from Harmony. Soon after our arrival home, I saw something which led me to the belief that the plates were placed or concealed in my father's barn. I frankly asked Joseph if my supposition was right, and he told me it was. Some time after this, my mother was going to milk the cows, when she was met out near the yard by the same old man (judging by her description of him) who said to her: "You have been very faithful and diligent in your labors, but you are tired because of the increase in your toil; it is proper therefore that you should receive a witness that your faith may be strengthened." Thereupon he showed her the plates. My father and mother had a large family of their own; the addition to it, therefore, of Joseph, his wife Emma, and Oliver very greatly increased the toil and anxiety of my mother. And although she had never complained, she had sometimes felt that her labor was too much, or at least she was perhaps beginning to feel so. This circumstance, however, completely removed all such feelings and nerved her up for her increased responsibilities.

Elder O. P. Have you any idea when the other record will be brought forth?

D. W. When we see things in the spirit and by the power of God they seem to be right here; the present signs of the times indicate the near approach of the coming forth of the other plates, but when it will be I cannot tell. The three Nephites are at work among the lost tribes and elsewhere. John the Revelator is at work, and I believe the time will come suddenly, before we are prepared for it.

Elder O. P. Have you in your possession the original MSS. of the Book of Mormon?

D. W. I have; they are in O. Cowdery's handwriting. He placed them in my care at his death, and charged me to preserve them as long as I lived; they are safe and well preserved.

J. F. S. What will be done with them at your death?

D. W. I will leave them to my nephew, David Whitmer, son of my brother Jacob, and my namesake.

O. P. Would you not part with them to a purchaser?

D. W. No. Oliver charged me to keep them, and Joseph said my father's house should keep the records. I consider these things sacred, and would not part with nor barter them for money.

J. F. S. We would not offer you money in the light of bartering for the MSS., but we would like to see them preserved in some manner where they would be safe from casualties and from the caprices of men, in some institution that will not die as man does.

D. W. That is all right. While camping around here in a tent, all my effects exposed to the weather, everything in the trunk where the MSS. were kept became mouldy, etc., but they were preserved, not even being discolored (we supposed his camping in a tent, etc., had reference to his circumstances after the cyclone, in June last). As he and others affirm, the room in which the MSS. were kept was the only part of the house which was not demolished, and even the ceiling of that room was but little impaired. "Do you think," said Philander Page, a son of Hiram Page, one of the eight witnesses, "that the Almighty cannot take care of his own?"

Next day (Sunday, September 8) Mr. Whitmer invited us to his house, where, in the presence of David Whitmer, Esq. (son of Jacob), Philander Page, J. R. B. Vancleave, David J. Whitmer (son of David the witness), George Schweich (grandson of David), Colonel Childs and others, David Whitmer brought out the MSS. of the Book of Mormon. We examined them closely and those who knew the handwriting pronounced the whole of them, excepting comparatively few pages, to be in the handwriting of Oliver Cowdery. It was thought that these few pages were in the handwritings of Emma Smith and John and Christian Whitmer.

We found that the names of the eleven witnesses were, however, subscribed in the handwriting of Oliver Cowdery. When the question was asked Mr.

Whitmer if he and the other witnesses did or did not sign the testimonies themselves, Mr. W. replied, "each signed his own name."

"Then where are the original signatures?"

D. W. I don't know; I suppose Oliver copied them, but this I know is an exact copy.

Someone suggested that he, being the last one left of the eleven witnesses, ought to certify to this copy. Lawyer D. Whitmer (Jacob's son) suggested that he had better reflect about it first and be very cautious.

J. F. S. suggested that perhaps there were *two copies* of the manuscripts, but Mr. Whitmer replied that, according to the best of his knowledge, there never was but the one copy. Herein, of course, he is evidently uninformed.

Elder O. Pratt again felt closely after the subject of procuring the MSS., but we found that nothing would move him on this point. The whole Whitmer family are deeply impressed with the sacredness of this relic. And so thoroughly imbued are they with the idea and faith that it is under the immediate protection of the Almighty that, in their estimation, not only are the MSS. themselves safe from all possible contingencies, but that they are a source of protection to the place or house in which they may be kept, and, it may be, to those who have possession of them.

III

STATEMENT IN KANSAS CITY "JOURNAL"

The following interview with David Whitmer was pub-lished in the Kansas City "Journal" under date of June 5, 1881, and subsequently published in the "Millennial Star," vol. 43, pp. 421-23 and 437-439.

IN VIEW of the large Mormon immigration that is now pouring into this county and also in view of the difficulties that have heretofore existed between that sect and the people of Jackson County, the *Journal* has taken the trouble to ascertain the facts as to the origin of the sect, as well as the history of their expulsion from Jackson County in 1833.

The translation of the Book is said to have been witnessed by eleven persons, as follows: Martin Harris, David Whitmer, Oliver Cowdery, Christian Whitmer, Hiram Page, Jacob Whitmer, Joseph Smith, Sr., Peter Whitmer, Jr., John Whitmer, Hyrum Smith, and Samuel H. Smith, all of whom except David Whitmer, are long since dead. David Whitmer, the only living witness, has resided since 1838 in Richmond, Ray County, Mo., and the *Jour-*

nal dispatched a reporter to Richmond to interview the "last of the eleven."

The reporter called at the residence of Mr. Whitmer and found the patriarch resting in an invalid's chair, looking very pale and feeble, he having but just recovered from a long and severe illness. In person, he is about medium height, of massive frame though not at all corpulent, his shoulders slightly bent as with the weight of years. His manly, benevolent face was closely shaven, his hair snow-white, and his whole appearance denoted one of nature's noblemen. The education acquired during his boyhood days and his long life devoted to study and thought have stored his mind with a vast fund of information.

After introducing himself, the reporter opened the conversation as follows:

"Mr. Whitmer, knowing that you are the only living witness to the translation of the Book of Mormon and also that you were a resident of Jackson County during the Mormon troubles in 1833, I have been sent to you by the *Journal* to get from your lips the true statement of facts in regard to these matters. For nearly half a century the world has had but one side only, and it is now our desire to present to our readers for the first time the other side."

"Young man, you are right. I am the only living witness to the Book of Mormon, but I have been imposed upon and misrepresented so many times by persons claiming to be honorable newspaper men, that I feel a delicacy in allowing my name to come before the public in newspaper print again."

"I am very sorry to hear that, but I promise you that we shall only give your statement as you make it and will not misrepresent you in any manner."

After a few other remarks of the same tenor the reporter at last induced the patriarch to furnish the desired facts, which he did in the following language:

"I was born near Harrisburg, Pa., January 7, 1805, but when only four years of age my parents removed to the state of New York, settling at a point midway between the northern extremities of Lake Cayuga and Seneca, two miles from Waterloo, seven miles from Geneva, and twenty-seven miles from Palmyra, where I lived until the year 1831. In the year 1830 I was married to Miss Julia A. Jolly who is still living. The fruit of our union was a son, David J. Whitmer, now aged 48, and a daughter, now aged 46 years, both of whom are now living with me.

"I first heard of what is now termed Mormonism in the year 1828. I made a business trip to Palmyra, N. Y., and while there stopped with one Oliver Cowdery. A great many people in the neighborhood were talking about the finding of certain golden plates by one Joseph Smith, Jr., a young man of the neighborhood. Cowdery and I, as well as many others, talked about the matter, but at that time I paid but little attention to it, supposing it to be only the idle gossip of the neighborhood. Cowdery said he was acquainted with the Smith family, and believing there must be some truth in the story of the plates, he intended to investigate the matter. I had conversation with several young men who said that Joseph Smith certainly had golden plates, and that before he had attained them he had promised to share with them, but had not done so and they were very much incensed with them. Said I, 'How do you know that Joe Smith has the plates?' They replied, 'We saw the place in the hill that he took them out of, just as he described it to us before he had obtained them.' These parties were so positive in their statements that I began to believe there must be some foundation for the stories then in circulation all over that part of the country. I had never seen any of the Smith family up to that time, and I began to inquire of the people in regard to them. I learned that one night during the year 1827, Joseph Smith, Jr., had a vision, and an angel of God appeared to him and told him where certain plates were to be found, pointing out the spot to him, and shortly afterward he went to that place and found the plates, which were still in his possession. After thinking over the matter for a long time, and talking with Cowdery, who also gave me a history of the finding of the plates, I went home.

"After several months Cowdery told me he was going to Harmony, Pa., whither Joseph Smith had gone with the plates on account of the persecutions of his neighbors, and see him about the matter. He did go, and on his way he stopped at my father's

house and told me that as soon as he found out anything, either truth or untruth, he would let me know.
After he got there he became acquainted with Joseph
Smith, and shortly after wrote to me telling me that
he was convinced that Smith had the records and
that he (Smith) had told him that it was the will of
heaven that he (Cowdery) should be his scribe to
assist in the translation of the plates. He went on,
and Joseph translated from the plates and he wrote
it down. Shortly after this, Cowdery wrote me another letter in which he gave me a few lines of what
they had translated, and he assured me that he knew
of a certainty that he had a record of a people that
inhabited this continent, and that the plates they
were translating gave a complete history of these people. When Cowdery wrote me these things and told
me that he had revealed knowledge concerning the
truth of them, I showed these letters to my parents,
brothers and sisters. Soon after, I received another
letter from Cowdery telling me to come down into
Pennsylvania and bring him and Joseph to my
father's house, giving as a reason therefor that they
had received a commandment from God to that
effect. I went down to Harmony and found everything just as they had written me. The next day
after I got there they packed up the plates and we
proceeded on our journey to my father's house, where
we arrived in due time, and the day after we commenced upon the translation of the remainder of the

plates. I, as well as all of my father's family, Smith's wife, Oliver Cowdery, and Martin Harris, were present during the translation. The translation was by Smith, and the manner as follows:

"He had two small stones of a chocolate color, nearly egg-shape and perfectly smooth, but not transparent,[1] called interpreters, which were given him with the plates. He did not use the plates in the translation, but would hold the interpreters to his eyes and cover his face with a hat, excluding all light, and before his eyes would appear what seemed to be parchment, on which would appear the characters of the plates in a line at the top and immediately below would appear the translation, in English, which Smith would read to his scribe, who wrote it down exactly as it fell from his lips. The scribe would then read the sentence written, and if any mistake had been made the characters would remain visible to Smith until corrected, when they faded from sight to be replaced by another line. The translation at my father's occupied about one month, that is from June 1 to July 1, 1829."

"Were the plates under the immediate control of Smith all the time?"

"No, they were not. I will explain how that was. When Joseph first received the plates he translated 116 pages of the book of Lehi, with Martin Harris as scribe. When this had been completed they rested

---

[1]This does not agree with the statement of Joseph Smith, who gives us the information that the stones were transparent.

for a time, and Harris wanted to take the manuscript home with him to show to his family and friends. To this Joseph demurred, but finally asked the Lord if Harris might be allowed to take it. The answer was 'No.' Harris teased Joseph for a long time and finally persuaded him to ask the Lord a second time, pledging himself to be responsible for its safe keeping. To this second inquiry the Lord told Joseph that Harris might take the manuscript, which he did, showing it to a great many people; but, through some carelessness, he allowed it to be stolen from him. This incurred the Lord's displeasure and He sent an angel to Joseph demanding the plates, and until Joseph had thoroughly repented of his transgressions, would not allow him to have the use of them again. When Joseph was again allowed to resume the translation, the plates were taken care of by a messenger of God, and when Joseph wanted to see the plates, this messenger was always at hand. The 116 pages of the book of Lehi which were stolen were never recovered, nor would the Lord permit Joseph to make a second translation of it.

"A few months after the translation was completed, that is in the spring of 1830, Joseph had the book published, and this (showing a well-worn volume) is a copy of the first edition, which I have had in my possession ever since it was printed."

"When did you see the plates?"

"It was in the latter part of June, 1829. Joseph, Oliver Cowdery and myself were together, and the angel showed them to us. We not only saw the plates of the Book of Mormon, but he also showed us the brass plates of the Book of Ether and many others. They were shown to us in this way: Joseph and Oliver and I were sitting on a log when we were overshadowed by a light more glorious than that of the sun. In the midst of this light, but a few feet from us, appeared a table upon which were many golden plates, also the sword of Laban and the directors. I saw them as plain as I see you now and distinctly heard the voice of the Lord declaring that the records of the plates of the Book of Mormon were translated by the gift and the power of God."

"Who else saw the plates at this time?"

"No one. Martin Harris, the other witness, saw them the same day, and the eight witnesses, Christian Whitmer, Hiram Page, Jacob Whitmer, Joseph Smith, Sen., Peter Whitmer, Hyrum Smith, Jno. Whitmer and Samuel H. Smith, saw them next day."

"Did you see the angel?"

"Yes, he stood before us. Our testimony as recorded in the Book of Mormon is absolutely true, just as it is written there."

"Can you describe the plates?"

"They appeared to be of gold, about six by nine inches in size, about as thick as parchment, a great many in number, and bound together like the leaves of a book by massive rings passing through the back edges. The engravings upon them were very plain and of very curious appearance. Smith made *fac-*

similes of some of the plates and sent them by Martin Harris to Professors Anthon and Mitchell, of New York City, for examination. They pronounced the characters reformed Egyptian, but were unable to read them."

"Did Joseph Smith ever relate to you the circumstances of his finding the plates?"

"Yes, he told me that he first found the plates in the year 1823; that during the fall of 1823 he had a vision, an angel appearing to him three times in one night and telling him that there was a record of an ancient people deposited in a hill near his father's house, called by the ancients 'Cumorah,' situated in the township of Manchester, Ontario County, N. Y. The angel pointed out the exact spot, and, some time after, he went and found the records or plates deposited in a stone box in the hill, just as had been described to him by the angel. It was some little time, however, before the angel would allow Smith to remove the plates from their place of deposit."

"When was the Church first established?"

"We had preaching during the time the book was being translated, but our Church was not regularly organized until after the book was printed in the winter of 1829-30. The first organization was in Seneca County, New York, under the name of 'The Church of Christ.' The first elders were Joseph Smith, Oliver Cowdery, Martin Harris, Hyrum Smith, John Whitmer, Peter Whitmer and myself. On the 6th of April, 1830, the Church was called

[83]

together and the elders acknowledged according to the laws of New York. Our instructions from the Lord were to teach nothing except the Old and New Testaments and the Book of Mormon.

"From that time the Church spread abroad and multiplied very rapidly. In the fall of 1830, Parley P. Pratt, Peter Whitmer, S. Peterson (and Oliver Cowdery) went to Kirtland, Ohio, and established a branch of the Church, which also grew very fast, and soon after a fine temple was erected, which is still standing.

"During the winter of 1830, the same parties went to Independence, Mo., established a church, and purchased very large tracts of land in all parts of Jackson County as well as a large amount of property in the town of Independence, including the site for the temple. The reason for the emigration to Jackson County was that Smith had received a revelation from God designating Independence as the place of the gathering of the Saints together in the latter days. Joseph Smith and Elder Sidney Rigdon, of the Kirtland church, established the church in Jackson County, but soon after returned to Ohio. The temple has never been built at Independence, but the site still remains vacant and the title deeds are held by the Church. I have no doubt but that at some future day it will be built.

"About 500 people emigrated from Ohio to Jackson County, and the Church there increased in numbers with extraordinary rapidity during the ensuing two years. They lived in peace in Jackson County until early in the summer of 1833, when difficulties arose between the Church and citizens of the county. What first occasioned these difficulties I am unable to say, except that the Church was composed principally of Eastern and Northern people who were opposed to slavery, and that there were among us a few ignorant and simple-minded persons who were continually making boasts to the Jackson County people that they intended to possess the entire county, erect a temple, etc. This of course occasioned hard feelings and excited the bitter jealousy of the other religious denominations.

"The Church at Independence established a newspaper called the *Morning and Evening Star,* which published the revelations and prophecies of Joseph Smith and the doctrines of the Church, and which also caused a great deal of hard feelings among the citizens.

"I was at that time living three miles east of Westport, and the first intimation I ever had that the people intended driving us out of the country was an affray between an organized mob of about eighty citizens and about eighteen Mormons, which occurred at Wilson's store, near Big Blue, about the middle of the summer of 1833. The mob destroyed a number of our dwellings and fired upon the little party of Mormons, killing one young man and wounding several others. The Mormons returned the fire, killing the leader of the mob, a Campbellite

[85]

preacher named Lovett. The next difficulty was in Independence, about the middle of July of the same year, when a large mob of armed men gathered in front of the Courthouse under the leadership, I think, of three men, named Wilson, Cockrell and Overton. A committee of ten was appointed to wait upon the leaders of the Church and state their demands, which were that the *Morning and Evening Star* newspaper office and all other places of business be closed and that we immediately leave the county. This was so sudden and unexpected that we asked time to consider the matter, which was refused, and a battle immediately ensued, during which the newspaper office, which stood on the southwest corner of the square, just south of the present site of Chrisman & Sawyer's bank, was torn down and the type scattered to the four winds. Bishop Partridge and another of the Saints were dragged from their houses and tarred and feathered upon the public square. Numerous other indignities were heaped upon us, but no one was killed.

"After this, difficulties of a like nature occurred almost daily, until some time in October when the final uprising took place and we were driven out at the muzzles of guns, from the county, without being given the opportunity of disposing of our lands. Our houses were burned and our property destroyed and several of our number killed. The indignities that were heaped upon us were simply terrible. We were beaten, our families grossly insulted, and we fled for our lives out of the county. We scattered in every direction, the larger portion going to Van Buren and Grand River. A short time after, the citizens of Clay County invited us to come there, which we did, and were treated with the utmost kindness."

"Did your people ever have an opportunity of selling their lands in Jackson County?"

"No, they did not, and it now by right belongs to their descendants."

IV

STATEMENT IN THE RICHMOND
(MISSOURI) "CONSERVATOR"

---

*The article reproduced below was written by David
Whitmer, and published in his home-town paper, the Richmond (Missouri) "Conservator," on March 25, 1881.*

UNTO ALL NATIONS, KINDREDS, TONGUES AND
PEOPLE, unto whom these presents shall come:

It having been represented by one John Murphy,
of Polo, Caldwell County, Missouri, that I, in a conversation with him last summer, denied my testimony
as one of the three witnesses of the Book of Mormon.

To the end, therefore, that he may understand
me now, if he did not then; and that the world may
know the truth, I wish now, standing as it were in the
very sunset of life, and in the fear of God, once and
for all to make this public statement:

That I have never at any time denied that testimony or any part thereof, which has so long since
been published with that book, as one of the three
witnesses. Those who know me best well know that I
have always adhered to that testimony. And that no
man may be misled or doubt my present views in re-

gard to the same, I do again affirm the truth of all my statements as then made and published.

"He that hath an ear to hear, let him hear;" it was no delusion; what is written is written, and he that readeth let him understand. * * *

"And if any man doubt, should he not carefully and honestly read and understand the same before presuming to sit in judgment and condemning the light, which shineth in darkness, and showeth the way of eternal life as pointed out by the unerring hand of God?"

In the Spirit of Christ, who hath said: "Follow thou me, for I am the life, the light and the way," I submit this statement to the world; God, in whom I trust, being my judge as to the sincerity of my motives and the faith and hope that is in me of eternal life.

My sincere desire is that the world may be benefited by this plain and simple statement of the truth.

And all the honor to the Father, the Son, and the Holy Ghost, which is one God. Amen!

DAVID WHITMER, SEN.
Richmond, Mo., March 19, 1881.

We, the undersigned citizens of Richmond, Ray County, Mo., where David Whitmer, Sen., has resided since the year A.D. 1838, certify that we have been long and intimately acquainted with him and know him to be a man of the highest integrity, and of undoubted truth and veracity.

[89]

Given at Richmond, Mo., this March 20, A.D. 1881.

A. W. Doniphan.

Geo. W. Dunn, Judge of the Fifth Judicial Circuit.

T. D. Woodson, President of Ray Co. Savings Bank.

J. T. Child, Editor of *Conservator*.

H. C. Garner, Cashier of Ray Co. Savings Bank.

W. A. Holman, County Treasurer.

J. S. Hughes, Banker, Richmond.

D. P. Whitmer, Attorney-at-law.

J. W. Black, Attorney-at-law.

L. C. Cantwell, Postmaster, Richmond.

Geo. I. Wasson, Mayor.

James A. Davis, County Collector.

C. J. Hughes, Probate Judge and Presiding Judge of Ray County Court.

Geo. W. Trigg, County Clerk.

W. W. Mosby, M.D.

Thos. McGinnis, ex-Sheriff, Ray County.

J. P. Quesenberry, Merchant.

W. R. Holman, Furniture Merchant.

Lewis Slaughter, Recorder of Deeds.

Geo. W. Buchanan, M.D.

A. K. Reyburn.

The *Conservator* also made the following editorial comments on the "notice."

Elsewhere we publish a letter from David Whitmer, Sen., an old and well known citizen of Ray, as well as an endorsement of his standing as a man, signed by a number of the leading citizens of this community, in reply to some unwarranted aspersions made upon him.

There is no doubt that Mr. Whitmer, who was one of the three witnesses of the authenticity of the gold plates, from which he asserts that Joe Smith translated the Book of Mormon (a facsimile of the characters he now has in his possession with the original records), is firmly convinced of its divine origin; and while he makes no effort to obtrude his views or belief, he simply wants the world to know that so far as he is concerned there is no "variableness or shadow of turning." Having resided here for nearly a half of a century, it is with no little pride that he points to his past record with the consciousness that he had done nothing derogatory to his character, as a citizen and a believer in the Son of Mary, to warrant such an attack on him, come from what source it may; and now, with the lilies of seventy-five winters crowning him like an aureole, and his pilgrimage on earth well-nigh ended, he reiterates his former statements, and will leave futurity to solve the problem that he was but a passing witness to its fulfillment.

V

STATEMENT OF JAMES H. MOYLE

David Whitmer, the last surviving member of the Three Witnesses of the Book of Mormon, died at Richmond, Missouri, January 25, 1888, 58 years ago. As far as it is known there is only one member of the Church now living who met David Whitmer and held an interview with him.

This member is James H. Moyle, a resident of the Cottonwood district in Salt Lake County, former president of the Eastern States Mission, former Commissioner of Customs of the United States and a distinguished citizen of Utah. Elder Moyle, now in his eighty-seventh year, remembers with interest his visit to Richmond, Missouri, in July, 1885. Elder Moyle relates that he was on his way to Salt Lake City after his graduation from the University of Michigan, and stopped off at Richmond to have a personal interview with David Whitmer. Elder Moyle's written account of this interview may be found in the Deseret News Church Section, August 2, 1944, and is as follows:

[Editor's Note: James H. Moyle died on February 19, 1946, while this volume was in course of publication.]

I WAS ALWAYS deeply interested in the Book of Mormon, and had been on a mission to the Southern States before I entered the University of Michigan. During my three years' residence at the University, I learned that David Whitmer was still living and in good health. I concluded to visit him on the way home to Salt Lake City. I graduated the latter part of June, 1885, and arrived in Richmond, Missouri, early in July.

Richmond is a small, rural town. I talked with the hack driver (that is what they called them) who took me to the hotel, and learned from him that David Whitmer was a highly respected citizen of the city. I likewise questioned the clerk of the hotel, with the same results. I made such inquiry as I could concerning him during my visit of part of a day.

I found David Whitmer seated under a fruit tree in front of his home, which was located near the street and surrounded by an orchard. I understood that he had been bothered a good deal by curiosity seekers, and to make him feel more at home with me, I presented him with an appropriate book. I said that I had just graduated as a law student and was on my way home, and was extremely anxious to obtain from him whatever he would be good enough to tell me about the Book of Mormon, the plates from which it was translated and his testimony concerning the same which he had given to the world.

I entered in a little diary which I kept the mere fact that I had visited David Whitmer and that he had verified all that had been published to the world concerning the Book of Mormon by him in his testimony, and that was about all. In making that visit I had no thought of anything but my personal knowledge and did not contemplate publishing anything concerning it — it was purely an individual matter

with me at the time. I told my friends about it and
spoke of it in the ward, but at that time it seemed to
be common knowledge. David Whitmer died about
three years after I saw him. My memory of the main
facts is perfectly clear. I have always enjoyed good
health, never better than at the present.

David Whitmer was a man above medium height,
slender rather than stout and was in his shirt-sleeves.
His hair was white. As I remember, he was a man
of fairly intellectual appearance, for the plain citizen
that he was, and of good countenance. I am quite
sure he was a serious-minded man.

I told him that I had been born in the Church,
my mother also; that my father had joined the
Church when he was a boy in his teens; that I had
grown up believing implicitly in the Book of Mormon; that I was about to commence life's activities
as he was getting ready to lay them down, and
pleaded with him to tell me the truth—not to permit
me to go through life believing in a falsehood—that
meant so much to me. I told him that he knew the
facts and urged him to tell me just what had happened in connection with the introduction of the Book
of Mormon. I seemed to gain his confidence and felt
free to ask him questions, and in fact did everything
that I could think of that would bring out the facts,
particularly all of the circumstances and details of
his seeing the angel, seeing and handling the plates
and where the interview with the Angel Moroni took

place and the conditions and circumstances surrounding the same.

He said that they (Joseph Smith, Oliver Cowdery, David Whitmer and Martin Harris) were out in the primitive woods in western New York; that there was nothing between them and the angel except a log that had fallen in the forest; that it was in the broad daylight with nothing to prevent either hearing or seeing all that took place. He then repeated to me that he did see and handle the plates; that he did see and hear the angel and heard the declaration that the plates had been correctly translated; that there was absolutely nothing to prevent his having a full, clear view of it all. I remember very distinctly asking him if there was anything unnatural or unusual about the surroundings or the atmosphere. He answered that question. I do not remember exactly the words he used, but he indicated that there was something of a haze or peculiarity about the atmosphere that surrounded them but nothing that would prevent his having a clear vision and knowledge of all that took place. He declared to me that the testimony which he had published to the world was true and that he had never denied any part of it.

I asked him why he had left the Church. He replied that he had never left the Church, that he had continued with the branch of the Church that was originally organized in Richmond and still presided over it. In answer to my questions, he said, in an unqualified, emphatic way, that Joseph Smith was a Prophet of God, but had become a fallen prophet through the influence which Sidney Rigdon exercised over him; that he accepted everything that was revealed to the Prophet down to the year 1835, but rejected everything thereafter because he did not know whether it came from the Lord or from Sidney Rigdon. He manifestly had become embittered against Sidney Rigdon due to his promotion to second place in the Church over men like himself who had been with the Prophet from the beginning and who had done so much for the Church. I then concluded, as I now believe, that jealousy and disappointment had soured his soul, but nothing could obliterate his testimony of the divinity of the Book of Mormon.

I asked him about the manuscript from which the Book of Mormon was published. He said that he had the original of the two copies that were made before the Book of Mormon was printed. I asked him if he would sell the manuscript. He said no. I then asked him if he wouldn't sell it at any price. He said no, that he would not part with it. He also said, pointing to his home, that when a cyclone struck Richmond a few years before, every room in his house was destroyed except the one in which that manuscript was kept. He seemed to regard the manuscript sacredly. As he appeared to be a poor man, at least in very ordinary circumstances, I was greatly impressed by the fact that he would not even talk about selling it and with the fact that he seemed to regard the care of the manuscript as being something of a sacred trust. Neither did he seek a reconciliation with the Church, although that would have inevitably increased his worldly comfort, and made him a highly honored personage among Latter - day Saints.

President Joseph F. Smith had previously interviewed him and had seen the manuscript. He said to me that it was not the original, but a copy made by Oliver Cowdery.

VI

STATEMENT OF EDWARD STEVENSON

The following interesting information is from the pen of Elder Edward Stevenson, a prominent missionary of pioneer days. The letter, dated February 16, 1886, and addressed to President Daniel H. Wells, may be found in the "Historical Record," page 211.

AFTER MY VISIT to Independence I took a run down to Lexington Junction, 42 miles from Kansas City, and up the Lexington Railroad five miles to Richmond, Ray County, Mo., and called on David Whitmer, desiring to see once more the only surviving witness of the visitation of the angel who commanded him with others to bear record of the truth of the coming forth of the Book of Mormon and this Gospel dispensation of the nineteenth century. Eight years ago I visited him, and 52 years ago I heard him bear his testimony, as also Oliver Cowdery and Martin Harris, when I was only a boy, 14 years of age, and I am a witness that each time their testimony has been by the power of God, that thrills through the whole system like a two-edged sword. David Whitmer is now just past 81 years of age and only by a hair's breadth has escaped from a deathbed. He is very feeble, his frame weighing less than one hundred pounds. In this, his last testimony, he said to me, "As sure as the sun shines and I live, just so sure did the angel appear unto me and Joseph Smith, and I heard his voice and did see the angel standing before us, and on a table were the plates, the sword of Laban, and the ball or compass." Although so weak and feeble, yet he fired up so that after a time I was necessarily obliged to check him and let him rest, while in turn I talked to him.

VII

ADDITIONAL TESTIMONY OF
DAVID WHITMER

The following excerpt is from a pamphlet written by David Whitmer and published by him in 1887, entitled, "Address to All Believers in Christ." The paragraphs given below are on page 8.

IT IS RECORDED in the *American Encyclopedia* and *Encyclopedia Britannica*, that I, David Whitmer, have denied my testimony as one of the three Witnesses of the Book of Mormon, and that the other two witnesses, Oliver Cowdery and Martin Harris, denied their testimony to that book.

I will say once more to all mankind, that I have never at any time denied that testimony or any part thereof. I also testify to the world that neither Oliver Cowdery nor Martin Harris ever at any time denied their testimony. They both died reaffirming the truth of the divine authenticity of the Book of Mormon.

DAVID WHITMER'S LAST HOURS—
STATEMENT IN RICHMOND
"DEMOCRAT"

David Whitmer's death occurred on January 25, 1888. At the time he was eighteen days past his eighty-third birthday. His last hours are well described in an article which appeared in his home-town paper, the Richmond "Democrat," under date of February 2, 1888. This article is reproduced herewith in part from the "Historical Record," by Andrew Jenson, pages 622-624.

DAVID WHITMER bore his long illness with great patience and fortitude, his faith never for a moment wavering, and when the summons came he sank peacefully to rest, with a smile on his countenance, just as if he was being lulled to sleep by sweet music. Just before the breath left the body, he opened his eyes, which glistened with the brightness of his early manhood. He then turned them towards heaven, and a wonderful light came over his countenance, which remained several moments, when the eyes gradually closed and David Whitmer had gone to his rest.

On Monday last (Jan. 23, 1888) at 10 o'clock a.m., after awakening from a short slumber, he said he had seen beyond the veil and saw Christ on the other side. His friends, who were constantly at his bedside, claim that he had many manifestations of the truths of the great beyond, which confirms their faith beyond all shadow of doubt.

On Sunday evening at 5:30 (Jan. 22, 1888) Mr. Whitmer called his family and some friends to his bedside, and addressing himself to the attending physician, said:

"Dr. Buchanan, I want you to say whether or not I am in my right mind, before I give my dying testimony."

The doctor answered: "Yes, you are in your right mind, for I have just had a conversation with you."

David Whitmer then addressed himself to all around his bedside in these words: "Now you must all be faithful in Christ. I want to say to you all, the Bible and the Record of the Nephites (Book of Mormon) are true, so you can say you have heard me bear my testimony on my deathbed. All be faithful in Christ, and your reward will be according to your works. God bless you all. My trust is in Christ forever, worlds without end. Amen."

On Friday morning last (Jan. 27, 1888) at 10:30 a.m., a number of the friends of the deceased assembled at his late residence, to pay a last tribute of respect to the worthy dead. Mr. John J. Snyder arose and read the first fourteen verses of the twenty-second chapter of Revelation, and stated that the deceased had selected the fourteenth verse to be read at the funeral service over his remains. It read as follows:

"Blessed are they that do his commandments, that they may have right to the tree of life, and may enter in through the gates into the city."

After reading, an appropriate eulogy was pronounced by John C. Whitmer, a relative and intimate associate of the deceased.

It was then announced that all present who desired to take a last look at the remains would be given an opportunity to do so at the house, as the coffin would not be opened at the grave. All present took advantage of this opportunity to look upon the features of the dead.

The following old and well-known citizens of Richmond acted as pallbearers: Joseph S. Hughes, Thomas D. Woodson, Dr. H. C. Garner, George L. Wasson, John B. Quissenberry and Col. J. W. Black, who then took charge of the remains and bore it to the hearse.

Notwithstanding the cold, damp weather, a large number of friends and acquaintances followed the hearse and mourning family to the new cemetery, west of the city, where the body was laid to rest, and all that was mortal of one of the most remarkable men ever connected with the history of Ray County was forever hidden from view.

David Whitmer lived in Richmond about half a century, and we can say that no man ever lived here who had among our people more friends and fewer enemies. Honest, conscientious and upright in all his dealings, just in his estimate of men, and open, manly and frank in his treatment of all, he made lasting friends who loved him to the end. He leaves a wife and two children, two grandchildren and several great-grandchildren.

Part Four

★ ★ ★ ★

MARTIN HARRIS

I

SKETCH OF THE LIFE OF
MARTIN HARRIS

This brief sketch of the life of Martin Harris has been gleaned from many sources. For a more extended account, see Jenson's "L.D.S. Biographical Encyclopedia," vol. 1, p. 271.

MARTIN HARRIS, one of the Three Witnesses of the Book of Mormon, was born on May 18, 1783, at Easttown, Saratoga County, New York. When in his ninth year he moved with his parents and brothers and sisters to a new, unsettled portion of western New York state, where a settlement called Palmyra was forming. Here he remained until 1831, during which time he acquired a farm of his own and became a prosperous, dependable citizen. He became acquainted with the family of Joseph Smith, Sr., after their settlement in Palmyra in 1816, and frequently hired the boy, Joseph, Jr., to work on his farm.

As an intimate acquaintance of the Smith family, he was early informed of the visions of Joseph Smith, Jr., and manifested a sincere interest in the wonderful events which were taking place in the life of the boy-Prophet. In the fall of 1827 he presented Joseph with fifty dollars to assist him "in doing the Lord's work."

Early in 1828 Martin visited Joseph at the latter's home in Harmony, Pennsylvania. Here he obtained a copy of some of the characters on the gold plates and took them to Charles Anthon, a professor of ancient languages in New York City, to learn the latter's opinion of the validity of the writings. The story is well-known regarding the manner in which Professor Anthon at first admitted that the characters were correct, and later repudiated his statement when he learned that Joseph Smith, Jr., had obtained the Ancient Records from an angel.

Returning to Harmony, Martin Harris became the young Prophet's scribe in the translation of the plates. The two worked diligently together from the middle of April, 1828, until the 14th of June following, during which time 116 pages had been written. Martin Harris then made the request of Joseph that he be permitted to carry the writings home and show them to his wife and certain of his relatives. At first Joseph deferred to this request, but after repeated importunings he was allowed to take the sacred manuscript, with the distinct provision that he would show it only to certain persons whom the Prophet named.

In this important transaction Martin Harris did not keep his word. He exhibited the writings promiscuously, and through his carelessness they were lost or destroyed. Tradition has it, in Palmyra, that the wife of Martin Harris, who was bitterly opposed to the work of the youthful Prophet, burned the manuscript, in order to sever the friendly relationship that existed between her husband and Joseph Smith, Jr.

However, although Martin Harris received a severe rebuke for his carelessness in losing the manuscript, he still continued to be friendly to the Prophet. When the translation of the Sacred Record was completed in the latter part of June, 1829, Martin Harris went from his home in Palmyra to the Whitmer home near Waterloo, a distance of twenty-five miles, to congratulate the Prophet on the successful conclusion of his great work. It was during this visit that he was permitted, in connection with David Whitmer and Oliver Cowdery, to behold the great vision in the grove near the Whitmer home, when the angel Moroni exhibited the plates to the witnesses and a voice from heaven declared that the translation had been correctly made.

After this vision Martin Harris became very enthusiastic about the work. He went with Joseph to a printer in Palmyra and mortgaged a part of his farm for $3,000 to pay for publishing 5,000 copies of the Book of Mormon. He was thus able to render material assistance when it was greatly needed.

The date when Martin Harris was baptized is not known, but the Prophet Joseph Smith informs us that it was very shortly after the Church was organized.

Early in 1831 Martin Harris left his home in Palmyra and went to Kirtland, Ohio, where the headquarters of the Church was located. In June of the same year he accompanied the Prophet and other Elders on a journey to Missouri. Shortly after their arrival, Jackson County was designated as the gathering place of the Saints and the site for the building of a temple was selected and dedicated.

Returning to Kirtland in the fall of 1831, Martin Harris proceeded to make that location his permanent home. In February, 1834, he was made a member of the Kirtland High Council, and one year later he assisted Oliver Cowdery and David Whitmer in selecting the members of the first quorum of Twelve Apostles, which task had been assigned by the Prophet to the Three Witnesses of the Book of Mormon. As long as the Saints remained in Kirtland, Martin Harris was active in the Church, but when the majority of the members moved away in 1838, Martin remained behind and gradually lost connection with the Prophet and later with President Brigham Young.

History tells us that shortly after the death of the Prophet, Martin Harris came under the influence of James J. Strang, an apostate from the Church who claimed to be the true successor to Joseph Smith. Under the influence of this man, Martin Harris went to England as a missionary for the Strangites in that country, but he soon saw that his task was hopeless and he left without accomplishing the object of his visit.

Returning to Kirtland, Martin Harris, who had been divorced from his first wife, was married to Caroline Young, daughter of John Young, and by her had several children. Sometime during the pioneer days, Caroline Young Harris left Kirtland and emigrated to Utah, leaving her husband, who refused to accompany her.

Martin Harris remained in Kirtland until 1870, when he was invited to come to Utah by Edward Stevenson, one of the First Council of Seventy, who was visiting in that neighborhood. Martin was eighty-seven years of age and was unable to raise enough money to purchase his ticket to Salt Lake City. The needed amount was furnished and on August 19th of that year, the aged witness of the Book of Mormon, accompanied by Elder Stevenson, began the journey to join his family in the valleys of the mountains.

Arriving in Salt Lake, Martin Harris was re-baptized by Elder Stevenson. He also addressed the Saints in the Tabernacle and visited among old friends whom he had known in the early days of the Church. His last years were spent at the home of his son, Martin Harris, Jr., in Clarkston, Cache County, Utah. Here he died on July 10, 1875, a few months after his ninety-second birthday. A granite pillar, designating him as one of the Three Witnesses of the Book of Mormon, now marks the site of his grave.

II

STATEMENT OF DAVID B. DILLE

The following statement was found in the files of the office of the "Millennial Star," in Liverpool, England, and was subsequently published in that paper (vol. 21, page 545). The records in the Historian's Office show that David B. Dille served as a missionary in the British Isles during 1853-54.

B E IT KNOWN to all whom this may concern that I, David B. Dille, of Ogden City, Weber County, Salt Lake, en route to Great Britain, having business with one Martin Harris, formerly of the Church of Latter-day Saints, and residing at Kirtland, Lake County, Ohio, did personally wait upon him at his residence, and found him sick in bed; and was informed by the said Martin Harris that he had not been able to take any nourishment for the space of three days. This, together with his advanced age, had completely prostrated him. After making my business known to Mr. Harris, and some little conversation with him, the said Martin Harris started up to bed, and, after particularly inquiring concerning the prosperity of the Church, made the following declaration: "I feel that a spirit has come across me—the old spirit of Mormonism; and I begin to feel as I used to feel; and I will not say I won't go to the Valley." Then addressing himself to his wife, he said, "I don't know but that, if you will get me some breakfast, I will get up and eat it."

I then addressed Mr. Harris relative to his once high and exalted station in the Church, and his then fallen and afflicted condition. I afterwards put the following questions to Mr. Harris, to which he severally replied with the greatest cheerfulness: "What do you think of the Book of Mormon? Is it a divine record?"

Mr. Harris replied and said, "I was the right-hand man of Joseph Smith, and I know that he was a Prophet of God. I know the Book of Mormon is true." Then smiting his fist on the table, he said, *"And you know that I know that it is true.* I know that the plates have been translated by the gift and power of God, for his voice declared it unto us; therefore I know of a surety that the work is true. For," continued Mr. Harris, "did I not at one time hold the plates on my knee an hour and a half, whilst in conversation with Joseph, when we went to bury them in the woods, that the enemy might not obtain them? Yes, I did. And as many of the plates as Joseph Smith translated I handled with my hands, plate after plate." Then describing their dimensions, he pointed with one of the fingers of his left hand to the back of his right hand and said, "I should think they were so long, or about eight inches, and about so thick, or about four inches; and each of the plates was thinner than the thinnest tin."

I then asked Mr. Harris if he ever lost 3,000 dollars by the publishing of the Book of Mormon. Mr. Harris said, "I never lost one cent. Mr. Smith," he said, "paid me all that I advanced, and more too." As much as to say he received a portion of the profits accruing from the sale of the book.

Mr. Harris further said, "I took a transcript of the characters of the plates to Dr. Anthon, of New York. When I arrived at the house of Professor Anthon, I found him in his office and alone, and presented the transcript to him, and asked him to read it. He said if I would bring the plates, he would assist in the translation. I told him I could not, for they were sealed. Professor Anthon then gave me a certificate certifying that the characters were Arabic, Chaldaic, and Egyptian. I then left Dr. Anthon and was near the door, when he said, 'How did the young man know the plates were there?' I said an angel had shown them to him. Professor Anthon then said, 'Let me see the certificate!'—upon which I took it from my waistcoat pocket and unsuspectingly gave it to him. He then tore it up in anger, saying there was no such thing as angels now—it was all a hoax. I then went to Dr. Mitchell with the transcript, and he confirmed what Professor Anthon had said."

Mr. Harris is about 58 years old [he was in reality 70 years old], and is on a valuable farm of 90 acres beautifully situated at Kirtland, Lake County, Ohio. (September 15, 1853)

[114]

III

STATEMENT OF WILLIAM H. HOMER

This interesting and faith-promoting account of a visit to Martin Harris, by William H. Homer, was published in the "Improvement Era" under date of March, 1926. The author at the time was eighty-one years of age and residing in Utah County.

I FIRST SAW Martin Harris in Kirtland, Ohio, about the last of December, 1869. On my return from a mission to England, I stopped to visit some of my relatives in Pennsylvania. On resuming my journey, one of my cousins, James A. Crockett, who was not a member of the Church, came as far as Kirtland, Ohio, with me. We remained in Kirtland over night, and the next morning after breakfast we asked the landlord who was custodian of the Mormon Temple at Kirtland, and he informed us that Martin Harris was custodian and pointed out to us where we would find the old gentleman. Accordingly we went to the door and knocked. In answer to our knock there came to the door of the cottage a poorly clad, emaciated little man, on whom the winter of life was weighing heavily. It was Martin Harris. In his face might be read the story of his life. There were the marks of spiritual upliftment. There were the marks of keen disappointment. There was the hunger strain for the peace, the contentment, the divine calm that it seemed could come no more into his life. It was a pathetic figure, and yet it was a figure of strength. For with it all there was something about the little man which revealed the fact that he had lived richly; that into his life had entered such noble experiences as come to the lives of but few.

I introduced myself modestly as a brother-in-law of Martin Harris, Jr.—as he had married my eldest sister — and as an Elder of the Church who was returning from a foreign mission. The effect of the introduction was electric. But the fact of relationship was overwhelmed by the fact of Utah citizenship. The old man bristled with vindictiveness. "One of those Brighamite Mormons, are you?" he snapped. Then he railed impatiently against Utah and the founder of the Mormon commonwealth. It was in vain that I tried to turn the old man's attention to his family. [Martin Harris was 86 years old at the time.] Martin Harris seemed to be obsessed. He would not understand that there stood before him a man who knew his wife and children; who had followed the Church to Utah.

After some time, however, the old man said, "You want to see the temple, do you?" "Yes, indeed," I exclaimed, "if we may." "Well, I'll get the key," he answered. From that moment, Martin Harris, in spite of occasional outbursts, radiated with interest.

[116]

He led us through the rooms of the temple and explained how they were used. He pointed out the place of the School of the Prophets. He showed where the temple curtain had at one time hung. He related thrilling experiences in connection with the history of the sacred building. In the basement, as elsewhere, there were many signs of delapidation; the plaster had fallen off the ceilings and the walls; windows were broken; the woodwork was stained and marred. Whether it was the influence of these conditions or not it is difficult to tell, but here again Martin Harris was moved to speak against the Utah Mormons. An injustice, a gross injustice had been done to him. He should have been chosen president of the Church.

When the old man was somewhat exhausted, I asked, "Is it not true that you were once very prominent in the Church; that you gave liberally of your means, and that you were active in the performance of your duties?" "That is very true," replied Martin. "Things were all right then. I was honored while the people were here, but now that I am old and poor it is all different . . ."

"What about your testimony to the Book of Mormon? Do you still believe that the Book of Mormon is true and that Joseph Smith was a prophet?" Again the effect was electric. A changed old man stood before me. He was no longer a man with an imagined grievance. He was a man with a message.

"Young man," answered Martin Harris with impressiveness, "Do I believe it? Do I see the sun shining? Just as surely as the sun is shining on us and gives us light, and the moon and stars give us light by night, just as surely as the breath of life sustains us, so surely do I know that Joseph Smith was a true prophet of God, chosen of God to open the last dispensation of the fulness of times; so surely do I know that the Book of Mormon was divinely translated. I saw the plates; I saw the angel; I heard the voice of God. I know that the Book of Mormon is true and that Joseph Smith was a true Prophet of God. 1 might as well doubt my own existence as to doubt the divine authenticity of the Book of Mormon, or the divine calling of Joseph Smith."

It was a sublime moment. It was a wonderful testimony. We were thrilled to the very roots of our hair. The shabby, emaciated little man before us was transformed as he stood before us with hand outstretched toward the sun of heaven. A halo seemed to encircle him. A divine fire glowed in his eyes. His voice throbbed with sincerity and the conviction of his message. It was the real Martin Harris, whose burning testimony no power on earth could quench. It was the most thrilling moment of my life.

I asked Martin Harris how he could bear such a wonderful testimony after having left the Church. He said, "Young man, I never did leave the Church; the Church left me."

Martin Harris was now in a softer mood. He turned to me and asked, "Who are you?" I explained again our relationship. "So my son Martin married your sister," repeated the old man, shaking my hand. "You know my family then?" "Yes," I replied. "Wouldn't you like to see your family again?" "I should like to see Caroline and the children," mused Martin, naming over the children, "but I cannot, I am too poor." "That need not stand in the way," I answered, "President Young would be only too glad to furnish means to convey you to Utah." "Don't talk Brigham Young," warned Martin, "he would not do anything that was right." "Send him a message by me," I persisted, now deeply concerned in the project. "No," declared Harris emphatically, "yet, I should like to see my family." "Then entrust me with a message," I pleaded. Martin paused. "Well," he said slowly, "I believe I will. You call on Brigham Young. Tell him about our visit. Tell him that Martin Harris is an old, old man, living on charity, with his relatives. Tell him I should like to visit Utah, my family and children—I would be glad to accept help from the Church, but I want no personal favor. Wait! Tell him that if he sends money, he must send enough for the round trip. I should not want to remain in Utah." For twenty-five years he had nursed the old grudge against the leaders of the Church, probably because nobody had had the patience with him that I had shown.

After we had bidden Martin Harris good-bye, and had taken a few steps from the temple, my cousin placed his hands on my shoulders and said, "Wait a minute." Looking me squarely in the eyes, he said,

"I can testify that the Book of Mormon is true. There is something within me that tells me that the old man told the truth. I know the Book of Mormon is true."

In due time I reached my home in the Seventh Ward in Salt Lake City. I recounted to my father my experiences with Martin Harris and we two set out immediately to report at the office of President Young. The president received us very graciously. He listened attentively to my recital of my visit to Martin Harris. President Young asked questions now and again to make clear certain points. Then, when the story was told, he said, and it seemed to me that he beamed with pleasure, "I want to say this: I was never more gratified over any message in my life. Send for him? Yes, even if it were to take the last dollar of my own. Martin Harris spent his time and money freely, when one dollar was worth more than one thousand dollars are now. Send for him? Yes, indeed, I shall send! Rest assured Martin Harris will be here in time. It was Martin Harris who gave the Prophet Joseph Smith the first money to assist in the translation of the Book of Mormon. Martin Harris was the first scribe to assist in the translation of the Book from the original plates, as dictated by the Prophet, who was led by the Holy Ghost. It was Martin Harris who was called, by revelation, to assist in the selection and ordination of the first Quorum of the Twelve Apostles of the newly organized Church. It was Martin Harris who was called upon to accompany the Prophet to Missouri to assist in the selection of the land of consecration. Martin Harris also aided in the selection of the first High Council of the Church, and he was a member of said Council. When the new Presidency of the Church was chosen, Martin felt greatly disappointed that he was not called to leadership, but Martin Harris never denied the faith, never affiliated with any other sect or denomination, but when the Church came west Martin remained behind. It is true that Martin Harris did not apostatize; he was never tried for his fellowship; he was never excommunicated."

During the summer of 1870, Elder Edward Stevenson was authorized to collect money by subscription to bring Martin Harris to Utah. About $200 was raised, and on August 30, 1870, Martin Harris arrived in Salt Lake City, in company with Elder Stevenson.

When Martin reached Salt Lake City, he visited Brigham Young at his home. They became reconciled and Martin Harris was invited to speak in the Tabernacle and he bore a faithful testimony. He went to Smithfield and later to Clarkston and made his home with his son, Martin Harris, Jr. In course of time he returned to full fellowship and communion with the Saints.

Early in July 1875, five years after he had come to Utah, Martin Harris was stricken with a kind of paralysis. It was the venerable witness' last illness, but through it all be remained true to the faith. At that time I and my small family lived in Clarkston.

With other members of the Clarkston Ward, I called at the Harris home to relieve them in the care of the old man. We began to think that he had borne his last testimony. The last audible words he had spoken were something about the Book of Mormon, but we could not understand what it was. But, these were not the aged witness' last words.

The next day, July 10, 1875, marked the end. It was in the evening—milking time—and Martin Harris, Jr., and his wife, Nancy Homer Harris, had gone out to milk and do the evening chores. In the house with the stricken man were left my mother, Eliza Williamson Homer, and myself, who had had so interesting a day with Martin Harris at Kirtland. I stood by the bedside holding the patient's right hand and my mother at the foot of the bed. Martin had been unconscious for a number of days. When we first entered the room the old gentleman appeared to be sleeping. He soon woke up and asked for a drink of water. I put my arm under the old gentleman, raised him, and my mother held the glass to his lips. He drank freely, and then he looked up at me and recognized me. He said, "I know you. You are my friend." He said, "Yes, I did see the plates on which the Book of Mormon was written; I did see the angel; I did hear the voice of God; and I do know that Joseph Smith is a Prophet of God, holding the keys of the Holy Priesthood."

This was the end. Martin Harris, divinely chosen witness of the work of God, relaxed, gave up my hand.   He lay back on his pillow, and just as the sun went down behind the Clarkston mountains, the spirit of Martin Harris passed on.   When Martin Harris, Jr., and his wife returned to the house, they found that their father had passed away, but in passing, Martin Harris, favored of God, repeated an unrefutable testimony of the divine inspiration and the prophetic genius of the great Prophet, Joseph Smith. (Signed, William Harrison Homer.)

IV

STATEMENT OF EDWARD STEVENSON

The following statement, originally written for the "Deseret News," was published in the "Millennial Star," vol. 44, pp. 78, 79, 86, and 87. The writer was a prominent member of the Church during pioneer days and a member of the First Council of Seventy from 1894 to 1896.

HAVING BEEN interrogated recently regarding Martin Harris, the time of his arrival in this city, and other incidents of his life, and as at the present newspaper reporters are interesting themselves regarding David Whitmer—the only surviving witness of the Book of Mormon, now living at Richmond, Ray County, Mo., having resided there as long as Martin Harris did at Kirtland, Ohio, which has been since 1831 (50 years ago), and 39 years previous to his removal to Utah—for these reasons I feel prompted to offer a few facts relating to his removal from Ohio to Utah, his various testimonies, and incidents of personal observation of his life for the past 48 years.

While I was living in Michigan, then a Territory, in 1833, near the town of Pontiac, Oakland County, Martin Harris came there, and in a meeting where I was present, bore testimony of the appearance of an angel exhibiting the golden plates and commanding him to bear a testimony of these things to all people, whenever opportunity was afforded him to do so; and I can say that his testimony had great effect in that vicinity. Martin had a sister living in our neighborhood. About this time Oliver Cowdery, one of the other three witnesses, also, in company with Joseph Smith the Prophet, bore the same testimony, and further, Joseph the Prophet promised those who with honest hearts obeyed the Gospel should receive the Holy Ghost, and signs would follow them. . . .

In the year 1869 I was appointed to a mission to the United States. Having visited several of the Eastern States, I called at Kirtland, Ohio, to see the first temple that was built by our people in this generation. While there, I again met Martin Harris, soon after coming out of the temple. He took from under his arm a copy of the Book of Mormon, the first edition, I believe, and bore a faithful testimony, just the same as that I heard him bear 36 years previously. He said that it was his duty to continue to lift up his voice, as he had been commanded to do, in defense of the Book that he held in his hand, and offered to prove from the Bible that just such a book was to come forth out of the ground—and that, too, in a day when there were no prophets on the earth— and that he was daily bearing testimony to many who visited the temple.

After patiently hearing him, I felt a degree of compassion for him, and in turn bore my testimony to him, as I had received it through obedience to the Gospel—that the work was still onward, and the words of Isaiah, second chapter, were being fulfilled; that the house of the Lord was "in the top of the mountains," and that under the leadership of President Brigham Young all nations were gathering to Zion to learn of God's ways and to walk in His paths; and that the worst wish that we had was for him to also prepare himself and go up and be a partaker of the blessings of the House of the Lord. My testimony impressed him. A Mr. Bond—who held the keys of the Temple, and who had been present at the dedication, and was then a faithful Latter-day Saint—said to me he felt as though he would have been far better off if he had kept with the Latter-day Saints, and that if I would preach in the Temple, he would open the doors to me. I promised to do so at some future time.

After my arrival in Utah in 1870, I was inspired to write to Martin Harris, and soon received a reply that the Spirit of God, for the first time, prompted him to go to Utah. Several letters were afterwards exchanged. President Brigham Young, having read the letter, through President G. A. Smith, requested me to get up a subscription and emigrate Martin to Utah, he subscribing twenty-five dollars for that purpose. Having raised the subscription to about $200, on the 19th of July, 1870, I took the railroad cars for Ohio, and on the 10th of August, filled my appointment, preaching twice in the Kirtland Temple, and finding Martin Harris elated with his prospective journey.

A very singular incident occurred at this time. While Martin was visiting his friends, bidding them farewell, his pathway crossed a large pasture in which he became bewildered, dizzy, faint and staggering through the blackberry vines that are so abundant in that vicinity. His clothes torn, bloody and faint, he lay down under a tree to die. After a time he revived, called on the Lord, and finally, at twelve midnight, found his friend, and in his fearful condition was cared for and soon regained his strength. He related this incident as a snare of the adversary to hinder him from going to Salt Lake City. Although in his 88th year he possessed remarkable vigor and health, having recently worked in the garden and dug potatoes by the day for some of his neighbors.

After visiting New York, and calling to visit the sacred spot from where the plates were taken, upon which the characters of the Book of Mormon were engraven, I found there an aged gentleman, 74 years old, who knew Martin Harris, and said that he was known in that neighborhood as an honest farmer, having owned a good farm three miles from that place. He further said he well remembered the time when the Mormons used to gather at Mormon Hill, as he termed it, where it was said the plates came from.

On the 21st of August, Martin was with me in Chicago, and at the American Hotel bore testimony to a large number of people of the visitation of the angel, etc. The following is from the Iowa *State Register*, Des Moines, August 26, 1870:

"Elder Stevenson, of Salt Lake, together with Martin Harris, one of the three witnesses of the Mormon Bible, called at our sanctum yesterday. Mr. Harris is now in his 88th year, hale and hearty, with many interesting things to relate in reference to the finding of the tablets of the testament. We shall have occasion to mention some of these in another issue."

While in Des Moines, the capital of Iowa, brother Harris had opportunity of bearing testimony to many. At a special meeting held in a branch of our Church (Brother James M. Ballinger, President), Brother Harris bore testimony as to viewing the plates, the angel's visit, and visiting professor Anthon with characters from the plates, who after giving him a certificate, etc., as to the correctness of the characters, asked him to fetch the plates for him to see. Martin said that they were sealed, and that an angel had forbidden them to be exhibited. Mr. Anthon then called for the certificate, tore it up and consigned it to the waste basket, saying that angels did not visit the earth in our day, etc.

On the following day I baptized a sister of President Ballinger, in the Des Moines River. The Branch here contributed a new suit of clothes to Brother Harris, for which he felt to bless them. On the 29th of August we landed in Ogden, and the Ogden *Junction* said:

"Martin Harris arrived [with Elder Edward Stevenson] whose name is known almost throughout the world as one of the witnesses of the Book of Mormon. They left Kirtland on the 19th of August."

August 31st, the *Salt Lake Herald* said:

"Martin Harris, one of the three witnesses of the Book of Mormon, arrived in Salt Lake City last night, accompanied by Elder Edward Stevenson. Two members of the Des Moines Branch of the Church accompanied them to our city."

The *Deseret News* of August 31, 1870, in over one column, notices the arrival of Martin Harris last evening, at 7:30: " . . . who is in his 88th year. He is remarkably vigorous for one of his years, his memory being very good, and his sight, though his eyes appear to have failed, being so acute that he can see to pick a pin off the ground. . . . He has never failed to bear testimony to the divine authenticity of the Book of Mormon. He says it is not a matter of belief on his part, but of knowledge. He with the other two witnesses declared, and their testimony has accompanied every copy of the book, that 'an angel of God came down from heaven, and brought and laid before our eyes, that we beheld and saw the plates, and the engravings thereon.' This declaration he has not varied from in 41 years. . . . We are glad to see Martin Harris once more in the midst of the Saints."

The *Salt Lake Herald*, September 3rd, said:

"We had a call yesterday morning from Elder Edward Stevenson, who introduced Martin Harris, one of the three witnesses to the Book of Mormon. Mr. Harris is now 88 years of age, and is remarkably lively and energetic for his years. He holds firmly to the testimony he has borne for over forty years—that an angel appeared before him and the other witnesses, and showed them the plates upon which the characters of the Book of Mormon were inscribed. After living many years separated from the body of the Church, he has come to spend the evening of life among the believers in that book to which he is so prominent a witness. Mr. Harris, who has a number of relatives in the Territory, came from the East under the care of Elder Edward Stevenson."

Monday Evening *News*, September 5, 1870, contains the following:

"SABBATH MEETINGS—The congregation in the morning was addressed by Elder Edward Stevenson, Martin Harris and President George A. Smith. In the afternoon the time was occupied by Elder John Taylor; the house was crowded to overflowing."

Martin Harris related an incident that occurred during the time that he wrote that portion of the translation of the Book of Mormon which he was favored to write direct from the mouth of the Prophet Joseph Smith. He said that the Prophet possessed a seer stone by which he was enabled to translate, as well as from the Urim and Thummim, and for convenience he then used the seer stone. Martin explained the translation as follows: By aid of the seer stone, sentences would appear and were read by the Prophet and written by Martin, and when finished he would say "Written," and if correctly written, that sentence would disappear and another appear in its place; but if not written correctly it remained until corrected, so that the translation was just as it was engraven on the plates, precisely in the language then used. Martin said that after continued translation they would become weary, and would go down to the river and exercise by throwing stones out on the river, etc. While so doing on one occasion, Martin found a stone very much resembling the one used for translating, and on resuming their labor of translation, Martin put in place the stone that he had found. He said that the Prophet remained silent, unusually and intently gazing in darkness, no traces of the usual sentences appearing. Much surprised, Joseph exclaimed, "Martin! What is the matter? All is as dark as Egypt!" Martin's countenance betrayed him, and the Prophet asked Martin why he had done so. Martin said, to stop the mouths of fools who had told him that the Prophet had learned those sentences and was merely repeating them, etc.

Martin said further that the seer stone differed in appearance entirely from the Urim and Thummim that was obtained with the plates, which were two clear stones set in two rims, very much resembling spectacles, only they were larger. Martin said there were not many pages translated while he wrote, after which Oliver Cowdery and others did the writing.

Brother Harris was taught the necessity of being rebaptized. He said that was new doctrine to him. Revelation, 2nd chapter, was explained—that those who had lost their first love and had fallen into evils and snares were called on to "repent and do their first works," and that rebaptism was a part of the Gospel. He claimed that he had not been cut off from the Church,* but said if that was required of him it would be manifested to him by the Spirit. Soon after his arrival in Utah he applied for baptism, saying that the Spirit had made known to him that it was his duty to renew his covenant before the Lord.

He was also taught a principle that was new to him—baptism for the dead, as taught and practiced by the ancient Saints, and especially taught by Paul the Apostle in the 15th chapter of 1st Corinthians: "Else what shall they do which are baptized for the dead, if the dead rise not at all? why are they then baptized for the dead?" After consideration he came and said it had been made known to him that baptism for the dead was a correct principle, for he had seen his father in vision at the foot of a ladder, and he was above and had to go down and help him up. In a short time the baptismal font was prepared, and by his request I baptized him, and President Geo. A. Smith and Apostles John Taylor, Wilford Woodruff,

*Note: Evidence recently found in the Historian's Office in Salt Lake City, would indicate that Martin Harris was excommunicated. See Journal History, January 1, 1938.

Jos. F. Smith and Orson Pratt confirmed him by the laying on of hands, Orson Pratt being mouth. As soon as he was confirmed he returned into the font and was baptized for several of his dead friends— fathers, grandfathers, etc. Then his sister also was baptized for the female relatives, and they were confirmed for and in behalf of those whom they were baptized for, by the same brethren, Jos. F. Smith being mouth. It was a time of rejoicing for all who were present.

Brother Martin visited many of the wards, continuing to bear his testimony both of what he had beheld with his own eyes, and verily knew to be true. He publicly said that many years ago, in Ohio, a number of persons combined and sought to get Martin to drink wine for the purpose of crossing him in his testimony. At the conclusion they asked him if he really believed the testimony that he had signed in the Book of Mormon to be true. He replied no, he did not believe it, but, much to their surprise, he said he *knew* it to be true!

Soon after receiving his blessings in the house of the Lord, he went to Smithfield, Cache Valley, and lived with his son until he left this mortal life. Just before he breathed his last he sat up in his bed, holding the Book of Mormon in his hand, and bore his last testimony to those who were present. (Salt Lake City, November 30, 1881)

V

ADDITIONAL STATEMENT OF EDWARD STEVENSON

In the "Millennial Star" of June 21, 1886, the following additional statement by Edward Stevenson was published. It contains valuable new material regarding Martin Harris.

THE ECONOMY OF Martin Harris was particularly illustrated on the occasion of our visit to the Fifteenth Ward of Salt Lake City. The meeting was crowded, as usual, with those anxious to see him, and to hear his constant, undeviating testimony. Sister M. H. Kimball, of the Fifteenth Ward, eminent in the Relief Society, on their behalf offered to have a new set of artificial teeth made for Brother Harris, to which he replied, "No, sisters, I thank you for your kindness, but I shall not live long. Take the money and give it to the poor." This calls to my mind a little incident or two that he related to me while we were on our journey from Ohio to Utah. He said that Joseph Smith, the Prophet, was very poor, and had to work by the day for his support, and he (Harris) often gave him work on his farm, and that they had hoed corn together many a day, Brother Harris paying him fifty cents per day. Joseph, he said, was good to work with and jovial and they often wrestled together in sport, but the Prophet was devoted and attentive to his prayers. Brother Harris gave Joseph $50 (10 pounds) on one occasion to help translate the Book of Mormon. This action on the part of Martin Harris so displeased his wife that she threatened to leave him. Martin said that he knew this to be the work of God, and that he should keep the commandments of the Lord, whatever the results might be. His wife, subsequently, separated from him, which he patiently endured for the Gospel's sake. . . .

At an evening visit of some of my friends at my residence in Salt Lake City, to see and hear Brother Harris relate his experience (which always delighted him) Brother James T. Woods, who is now present while I am writing this article, reminds me that himself and G. D. Keaton were present on that occasion, and asked him to explain the manner in which the plates containing the characters of the Book of Mormon were exhibited to the witnesses. Brother Harris said that the angel stood on the opposite side of the table on which were the plates, the interpreters, &c., and took the plates in his hands and turned them over. To more fully illustrate this to them, Brother Martin took up a book and turned the leaves over one by one. The angel declared that the Book of Mormon was correctly translated by the power of God and not of man, and that it contained the fullness of the Gospel of Jesus Christ to the Nephites, who were a branch of the lost sheep of the House of Israel, and had come from the land of Jerusalem to America. The witnesses were required to bear their testimony of these things, and of this open vision to all people, and he (Harris) testified, not only to those present but to all the world, that these things were true, and before God whom he expected to meet in the day of judgment he lied not. Brother Woods testifies that he was present at the time above mentioned, and to him it was marvelous to see the zeal that was manifested by Martin Harris, and the spirit of the Lord that accompanied his words.

That Martin Harris was very zealous, somewhat enthusiastic, and what some would term egotistical, is no doubt the case; but the Lord has shown this generation that He can carry on His work independently of all men, only as they live closely and humbly before Him. I will give one or two instances of Martin's enthusiasm. When President George A. Smith and others of us were being driven by John Henry Smith in a carriage to take a bath in the Warm Springs, near Salt Lake City, while passing over a high hill, President Smith directed the curtains of the carriage to be raised, giving a magnificent view of the city below. The immense Tabernacle and the Temple—and in fact the beautiful city in full view— looked wonderful to Brother Harris, who seemed wrapped in admiration and exclaimed, "Who would have thought that the Book of Mormon would have done all this?" On one occasion while celebrating a baptism, several persons being in attendance, Brother Harris with joyful feelings said, "Just see how the Book of Mormon is spreading." Having been absent so long from the body of the Church and considering his great age, much charity was necessary to be exercised in his behalf. His abiding testimony, and his assistance with his property to publish the Book of Mormon, have earned a name for him that will endure while time shall last.

Soon after he had received his endowments and performed some work for his dead, he retired to live with his son, Martin Harris, Jr., at Smithfield in Cache Valley, where he was comfortably cared for in his declining old age. On the afternoon of his death he was bolstered up in his bed, where, with the Book of Mormon in his hand, he bore his last testimony to those who were present. Brother Harris was over ninety years of age at the time of his death, and had always enjoyed good health. Bishop Rigby, who preached his funeral sermon, placed the Book of Mormon on his breast, while he lay in his coffin, and it was buried with him. (Signed, Edward Stevenson.)

VI

DEATH OF MARTIN HARRIS

Under date of July 17, 1875, the following article appeared in the "Deseret Evening News." It contains a short account of the life of Martin Harris and the details of his death and funeral.

MARTIN HARRIS, who departed this life on July 10, 1875, was, in a very peculiar manner, a man highly favored of God—a man favored with beholding an angel from heaven in his glory, holding in his hands ancient sacred records on plates of gold. He was an American by birth, born on the 18th of May, 1783, in Easttown, Saratoga County, New York. He removed to Palmyra, N. Y., where he became acquainted with Joseph Smith, Jun., the translator of the Book of Mormon. This great Prophet of the last days, having copied some of the ancient characters from gold plates which he had found, and translated them, presented them to Martin Harris, who made a visit to New York City, and showed the characters to the celebrated Professor Anthon, skilled in ancient and modern languages. The learned professor, after his examination, spoke favorably of the characters and of the translation, and proffered his assistance; but on learning from Mr. Harris that the book was discovered to Joseph Smith by an angel, and that a part of the Book was sealed, and that the finder was forbidden to let the Book go into the hands of the public, he sarcastically remarked that he could "not read a sealed book." Mr. Harris returned and reported to Mr. Smith the results of his interview with the "learned"; after which Mr. Smith, being commanded of the Lord, commenced translating the Book by the aid of the Urim and Thummim. Martin Harris was his first scribe and wrote 116 pages of manuscript, from the Prophet's mouth.

In the year 1829, Martin Harris, in company with the Prophet, and Oliver Cowdery and David Whitmer, retired to a grove, not far from Mr. Whitmer's farmhouse, in Fayette, Seneca County, New York, and called upon the Lord one by one; after which an angel descended from heaven in great glory, and showed them the plates, and the engravings upon the same, and at the same time they heard the voice of the Lord out of the heavens, bearing witness of the correctness of the translation, and commanding them to bear testimony of the same to all nations. (For their testimony see all the editions of the Book of Mormon in different languages.)

When the Prophet finished the translation, Martin Harris furnished $3,000 towards the publication of the first edition.

When, by the commandment of the Lord, the Church was organized in April, 1830, Martin Harris was among the first to identify himself with the baptized Saints.

When Jackson County, Mo., in 1831, was designated as a gathering place for the Saints, as the land upon which the New Jerusalem should be built, and where a full consecration of all properties should be required, and the holy United Order of God should be established, Martin Harris was the first one called of God by name to set an example before the Church in laying his money before the Bishop.

Notwithstanding these great favors shown to this remarkable man he had, like all of Adam's race, his imperfections. He did not follow up his brethren in all their persecutions in the states of Missouri and Illinois, but remained for many years in Ohio; this gave rise to many conjectures that Mr. Harris had apostatized. But it can truly be said that Mr. Harris never faltered nor swerved in the least degree from the great testimony given in the Book of Mormon.

Mr. Harris, a few years ago, emigrated to Utah, and like all other emigrating Saints, he, in this Territory, renewed his covenants by rebaptism; and also went into the font and was baptized for and in behalf of many of his kindred who were dead.

He located in Cache County, and continued to bear a faithful testimony to the divinity of the Book of Mormon up to his last moments. Being nearly 93 years of age, it may truly be said he fell asleep of old age. A few hours before his death, when prostrated with great weakness, Bishop Simon Smith came in. Mr. Harris stretched forth his hands to salute him and said, "Bishop, I am going." His son says: "The Bishop told father that he had something of importance to tell him in relation to the publishing of the Book of Mormon in the Spanish language, by the request of the Indians in Central America. Upon learning this, father brightened up, and his pulsation improved, and although very weak, he began to talk as he formerly had done previous to his sickness, and I think that he spoke about two hours, so that you may see by this that the mere mention of the Book of Mormon seemed to put new life into him."

His Illness and Funeral

From a letter from Martin Harris, Jr., to President Geo. A. Smith, dated Clarkston, Cache County, July 9th, we glean the following particulars of the last illness of Martin Harris:

"I and my family are all well, except my father, and he is very sick at the present time. He is so sick and weak that he cannot sit up in bed. He has no appetite, and has scarcely eaten anything for about a week. About the only thing he will now take is a little cold water, and he does not ask for that, but we give him a little as often as we think that he is able or willing to take it. He was taken sick a week ago yesterday, with some kind of a stroke, or life became so weak and exhausted that he has no use in his limbs. He cannot move, only by our aid. He has continued to talk a little every day till today, but now his voice is nearly inaudible. We think that he is gradually failing, and that he cannot live much longer, unless some great change for the better takes place. He has continued to talk about and testify to the truth of the Book of Mormon, and was in his happiest mood when he could get somebody to listen to his testimony; if he felt dull and weary at times, and someone would come in and open up a conversation and give him an opportunity of talking, he would immediately revive and feel like a young man for a little while. We begin to think that he has borne his last testimony. The last audible words he has spoken were something about the three witnesses of the Book of Mormon, but we could not understand what it was."

His son writes: "We had a good attendance and a large turn-out for a small town like Clarkston. Every respect that could be paid to him was manifested by the people. . . . We put the Book of Mormon in his right hand, and the Book of Doctrine and Covenants in his left hand. We had a very good coffin, and finished very nicely. We inscribed on the headboard the following: his name, and birth, and age, and place of birth, and also his death, with the words—'One of the Three Witnesses of the Book of Mormon,' also their testimony."

There were 16 teams or wagons, well filled with the people, who entertained a kind regard for old brother Martin.

Part Five

★ ★ ★ ★

SHORT SKETCHES OF THE LIVES OF THE EIGHT WITNESSES OF THE BOOK OF MORMON

*As they were written and published
by Andrew Jenson in the year 1888.*

I

CHRISTIAN WHITMER

ONE OF THE eight witnesses to the Book of Mormon was the eldest son of Peter Whitmer, Sen., and Mary Musselman, and was born January 18, 1798, in Pennsylvania. He removed while quite young, with his parents, from Pennsylvania to Seneca County, western New York, where he married Anne Schott, February 22, 1825.

He was among the number who first embraced the fullness of the gospel as revealed through the youthful Prophet, and was baptized, together with his wife in Seneca Lake, April 11, 1830, by Elder Oliver Cowdery. This was only five days after the Church was organized. As early as June, 1830, he held the office of Teacher in the Church and was ordained an Elder in 1831. In that year he removed with the rest of the Whitmer family and the Saints generally from New York State to Ohio, and the following year to Jackson County, Mo., where, at a council meeting held September 15, 1832, he was appointed to preside over the Elders in Jackson County. In a council of High Priests held August 21, 1833, he was ordained a High Priest by Simeon Carter. He passed through all the scenes of persecutions and mobbings which took place in that part of the country until, in connection with the rest of the Saints, he was driven out of Jackson County in November, 1833. He settled temporarily in Clay County, where he was chosen as one of the High Councilors of the Church in Missouri, July 3, 1834. This position he occupied until his death, which occurred in Clay County, November 27, 1835.

He was faithful and true until the last, and always bore a strong testimony of the divinity of the Book of Mormon. He left no children. After his demise his wife returned to her parents in New York State, where she married again, but was later divorced from her second husband. She died many years ago in Seneca County, New York. (See *L.D.S. Biographical Encyclopedia,* by Jenson, vol. 1, pages 276-283)

II

JACOB WHITMER

ONE OF THE eight witnesses to the Book of Mormon, was the second son of Peter Whitmer, Sen., and Mary Musselman, and was born in Pennsylvania January 27, 1800. He removed with his parents to New York State when a boy, and married Elizabeth Schott, September 29, 1825. They became the parents of nine children, of whom only two were alive in the year 1888.

Jacob Whitmer was one of the first of his father's family to become convinced that the principles revealed by the Prophet Joseph Smith were true, and, together with his wife, he was baptized by Oliver Cowdery, in Seneca Lake, April 11, 1830, a few days after the Church was organized. With the other members of the Whitmer family he removed to Ohio in 1831, and subsequently settled in Jackson County, Mo., from whence he was driven by a mob in 1833. He was also identified with the Church in Clay and Caldwell counties. In the latter county he acted a short time as a temporary High Councilor and also as a member of the building committee for the erection of the Lord's House at Far West.

He severed his connection with the Church in 1838, after which he settled near Richmond, Ray

[147]

County, where he remained until his death on April 21, 1856. He was 56 years, 2 months and 26 days old at the time of his demise. He was a shoemaker by trade and also owned a small farm.

One of his sons, David P. Whitmer, was a lawyer of considerable prominence and served one or more terms as mayor of Richmond. One of his daughters, Mrs. Mary Ann Bisbee, widow of the late J. P. Bisbee, lived in 1888 near Richmond, Mo., and had been a widow for a number of years. John C. Whitmer, his only remaining son, also lived about a mile south of Richmond in 1888. He was then the custodian of the original Church record which his uncle John Whitmer refused to give up to the proper authorities, and he also presided over the so-called "Whitmer Faction," or the Church of Christ, which accepts some of the doctrines taught by the Prophet Joseph Smith.

John C. Whitmer testified to Elder Andrew Jenson in September, 1888, as follows: "My father (Jacob Whitmer) was always faithful and true to his testimony in regard to the Book of Mormon, and confirmed it on his deathbed." From other sources it is known that Jacob Whitmer ever remained firm and steadfast to his testimony of the divinity of that Sacred Record. (See *L. D. S. Biographical Encyclopedia*, vol. 1, p. 276)

III

PETER WHITMER, JUNIOR

ONE OF THE eight witnesses to the Book of Mormon was the fifth son of Peter Whitmer, Sen., and Mary Musselman, and was born September 27, 1809, in Fayette, Seneca County, New York. Soon after Joseph's arrival at Fayette from Pennsylvania in the summer of 1829, Peter became a zealous friend of the Prophet and an able assistant in the translation of the Book of Mormon. He earnestly desired that Joseph would inquire of the Lord for him in order that he might know his duties and the Lord's will concerning him. The Prophet did so through the Urim and Thummim, and received a revelation commanding Peter to preach repentance to this generation (Doc. and Cov., Sec. 16). This was in June, 1829. About the same time he was baptized by Oliver Cowdery in Seneca Lake, being at that time less than twenty years of age.

In September, 1830, he was called by revelation (Doc. and Cov., Sec. 30) to preach the gospel, together with Oliver Cowdery, and in the following month he was chosen by revelation to accompany Parley P. Pratt, Oliver Cowdery and Ziba Peterson on a mission to the Lamanites (Doc. and Cov., Sec. 32). They started for the West soon afterwards, and had an eventful journey, fraught with many hardships and much suffering. In Kirtland, Ohio, they raised up a large branch, after which they traveled nearly one thousand miles through mud and snow, mostly on foot, to Jackson County, Missouri, where they arrived in the early part of 1831. While Parley P. Pratt and Oliver Cowdery commenced a mission among the Lamanites across the borders, Peter Whitmer, Jun., and another missionary companion, found employment as tailors in the town of Independence, remaining there until the arrival of Joseph Smith and a number of the brethren in July following. Subsequently Peter Whitmer, Jun., took an active part with the Saints in Jackson County, where he was ordained a High Priest October 25, 1831, by Oliver Cowdery. He suffered together with the rest of the Saints during the Jackson County persecutions in 1833, and was among those who found a temporary home in Clay County.

He took sick and died on a farm about two miles from Liberty, Clay County, September 22, 1836, and was buried by the side of his brother Christian, who had died about ten months previously. He had been ill for a number of years previous to his demise. He left a wife and three children, all daughters, one of them being born after his death. Like all the other witnesses to the Book of Mormon, Peter Whitmer, Jun., was true and faithful to his testimony until his death. (See *L. D. S. Biographical Encyclopedia*, vol. 1, p. 277)

IV

JOHN WHITMER

THE THIRD SON of Peter Whitmer, Sen., and Mary Musselman, was born August 27, 1802. He was baptized by Oliver Cowdery in Seneca Lake in June, 1829, soon after Joseph Smith's arrival in Seneca County from Pennsylvania. His brothers David and Peter were baptized about the same time.

John Whitmer assisted Joseph Smith and Oliver Cowdery considerably in writing while they were translating the latter part of the Book of Mormon in his father's house. In the meantime he became very zealous in the work, and, according to his earnest desire, Joseph inquired concerning him through the Urim and Thummim, and received a revelation in which he was commanded to declare repentance and bring souls unto Christ (Doc. and Cov., Sec. 15). He was closely connected with the Prophet in his early administrations, and accompanied him on his first missionary trips to Colesville, Broome County, where a large branch of the Church was built up in the midst of considerable persecution. He was also present at the little meeting at Harmony, Pennsylvania, in August, 1830, when the revelation concerning the Sacrament was given (Doc. and Cov., Sec. 27).

In September, 1830, he was called by revelation to preach the gospel and to labor continuously in the interest of Zion (Doc. and Cov., Sec. 30), and on March 8, 1831, he was chosen by revelation to labor as a historian for the Church (Doc. and Cov., Sec. 47). Again in November, 1831, he was called by revelation (Doc. and Cov., Sec. 69) to accompany Oliver Cowdery to Jackson County, Missouri, with the revelations which he had previously assisted Joseph in copying and preparing for printing. He was also one of the "seven High Priests sent up from Kirtland to build up Zion," to stand at the head of the Church in Jackson County, Missouri, and at the time of the persecutions was a member of the committee who negotiated with the mob and agreed that the Saints should leave Jackson County. Later we find his name attached to petitions addressed to Governor Dunklin, of Missouri, praying for redress and protection against mob violence. In Clay County he was again quite active and his name appears in connection with several important documents and in the correspondence of the Church at that time. Next to his brother David, John was the most prominent and able man among the Whitmers, and rendered efficient service to the Church in various ways, as long as he remained faithful. July 3, 1834, he was ordained one of the assistant-presidents of the Church in Clay County, his brother David being ordained president on the same occasion. Some time afterwards John paid a visit to Kirtland, Ohio, where he acted as a High Councilor and took an active part in the affairs of the Church as one of the presiding officers from Missouri. He was present at the dedication of the Kirtland Temple, and received his blessings and anointings under the hands of the First Presidency, after which he returned to Missouri. At a meeting of High Priests held in Far West, Missouri, April 7, 1837, he was appointed to act as a member of a committee for the sale of town lots in Far West.

At a conference held in Far West, November 7, 1837, objections were made to John Whitmer as one of the assistant-presidents of the Church in Missouri, but after he had made confessions he was temporarily sustained in his position. On February 5, 1838, however, he was finally rejected, together with his brother David Whitmer and William W. Phelps, the other two presidents of the Church in Missouri. John was excommunicated from the Church by the High Council at Far West, March 10, 1838, "for persisting in un-Christian-like conduct."

After his excommunication from the Church, John Whitmer refused to deliver the Church documents in his possession to the proper authorities, which gave occasion for quite a severe letter from Joseph Smith and Sidney Rigdon. The records, however, were never obtained; they are now (1888) in the custody of John C. Whitmer (a nephew of John Whitmer), who resides in Richmond, Missouri.

After the fall of Far West, John took advantage of the cheap rates at which the lands, that the

Saints were compelled to leave, could be bought, and succeeded in purchasing the principal part of the old townsite. When he died at his residence at Far West, July 11, 1878, he was known as an extensive farmer and stock-raiser. Although he never joined the Church again, after his excommunication in 1838, he was always true to his testimony in regard to the Book of Mormon. Even in his darkest days, and at the time he first turned his back upon the Church and the Prophet Joseph, he declared in the presence of a number of Missourians—enemies to the work of God — that he knew the Book of Mormon was true. His nephew, John C. Whitmer, of Richmond, Ray County, Missouri, who was with him a few days before his death, testifies that he bore testimony to the truth of the Book of Mormon until the last, which is corroborated by many others who visited him on various occasions previous to that time.

John Whitmer was the father of four children, three sons and one daughter. One of his sons died when about ten years old and another was killed in the Civil War. His only remaining son, Jacob D. Whitmer, lived on the old Far West site, and owned one of the best farms in that part of the country, including the Temple Block, which he inherited from his father. John's only daughter also lived in Far West, on the old homestead, a little east of Jacob D. Whitmer's residence. (See *L. D. S. Biographical Encyclopedia,* vol. 1, p. 251)

V

HIRAM PAGE

O NE OF THE eight witnesses to the Book of Mormon, was born in the state of Vermont in the year 1800. He commenced the study of medicine when quite young, and later traveled considerably in the state of New York and in Canada as a physician. Finally he located in Seneca County, N. Y., where he became acquainted with the Whitmer family, and finally married Catherine Whitmer (a daughter of Peter Whitmer and Mary Musselman) November 10, 1825. Nine children were born to them.

Having become a firm believer in the fulness of the gospel as revealed through the Prophet Joseph, he was baptized by Oliver Cowdery, in Seneca Lake, on April 11, 1830. His wife was baptized at the same time. Soon afterwards he came in possession of a stone by which he obtained certain revelations concerning the order of the Church and other matters, which were entirely at variance with the New Testament and the revelations received by Joseph Smith. This happened at a time when Joseph was absent, and when he heard of it, it caused him much uneasiness, as a number of the Saints, including Oliver Cowdery and the Whitmer family, believed in the things revealed by Hiram Page. At a conference held in September, 1830, when Joseph presided, this matter was given close attention, and after considerable investigation Hiram Page, as well as all the other members who were present, renounced everything connected with the stone.

In 1831, Hiram Page removed to Kirtland, Ohio, where he remained until the following year, when he settled in Jackson County, Missouri, near the town of Independence. During the persecutions of the Saints in Jackson County in 1833, he was selected, together with three others, to go to Lexington to see the circuit judge and obtain a peace warrant. Upon their affidavits, Judge John F. Ryland issued writs against some of the ringleaders of the mob, to be placed in the hands of the Jackson County sheriff, but these writs never accomplished any good. After the expulsion from Jackson County, Brother Page took an active part with the Saints in Clay County, and in 1836 he became one of the founders of Far West, Caldwell County.

In 1838 he severed his connection with the Church and subsequently removed to Ray County, where he remained until the end of his earthly career. He died August 12, 1852, on his farm near the present site of Excelsior Springs, about fourteen miles northwest of Richmond, Ray County, Mo., and near the boundary line between Ray and Clay counties. Of his nine children only four were living in 1888. His eldest living son, Philander Page, resided at that time two and a half miles south of Richmond. Another son lived nearby, and a daughter resided in Carroll County, Missouri.

Philander Page testified to Elder Andrew Jenson in September, 1888, as follows: "I knew my father to be true and faithful to his testimony of the divinity of the Book of Mormon until the very last. Whenever he had an opportunity to bear his testimony to this effect, he would always do so, and seemed to rejoice exceedingly in having been privileged to see the plates and thus become one of the eight witnesses. I can also testify that Jacob, John and David Whitmer and Oliver Cowdery died in full faith in the divinity of the Book of Mormon. I was with all these witnesses on their deathbeds and heard each of them bear his last testimony."

John C. Whitmer, a nephew of Hiram Page by marriage, testified in the presence of Elder Jenson: "I was closely connected with Hiram Page in business transactions and other matters, he being married to my aunt. I knew him at all times and under all circumstances to be true to his testimony concerning the divinity of the Book of Mormon." (See *L .D. S. Biographical Encyclopedia*, vol. 1, p. 277)

VI

JOSEPH SMITH, SENIOR

T HE FIRST Presiding Patriarch of the Church of Jesus Christ of Latter-day Saints, and father of the Prophet Joseph Smith, was born July 12, 1771, in Topsfield, Essex County, Mass. He was the second of the seven sons of Asahel and Mary Smith. Asahel was born in Topsfield, March 7, 1744; he was the youngest son of Samuel and Priscilla Smith. Samuel was born January 26, 1714, in Topsfield; he was the eldest son of Samuel and Rebecca Smith. Samuel was born in Topsfield, January 26, 1666, and was the son of Robert and Mary Smith, who emigrated from Old England.

Joseph Smith, Sen., removed with his father to Tunbridge, Orange County, Vermont, in 1791, and assisted in clearing a large farm of a heavy growth of timber. He married Lucy, daughter of Solomon and Lydia Mack, on January 24, 1796, by whom he had 10 children, namely:

Alvin	Born February 11, 1798
Hyrum	Born February 9, 1800
Sophronia	Born May 16, 1803
Joseph	Born December 23, 1805
Samuel Harrison . .	Born March 13, 1808
Ephraim	Born March 13, 1810

William	Born March 13, 1811
Catherine	Born July 28, 1812
Don Carlos	Born March 25, 1816
Lucy	Born July 18, 1821

At his marriage he owned a substantial farm in Tunbridge. In 1802 he rented it and engaged in the mercantile business, and soon after embarked in a venture of ginseng to send to China, and was swindled out of the entire proceeds by the shipmaster and agent; he was consequently obliged to sell his farm and all of his effects to pay his debts.

About the year 1816 he moved to Palmyra, Wayne County, New York, bought a farm and cleared 100 acres, which he lost in consequence of not being able to pay the last instalment of the purchase price at the time it was due. This was the case with a great number of farmers in New York who had cleared land under similar contracts. He afterwards moved to Manchester, and later to Waterloo, New York, where he lived until he removed to Kirtland, Ohio.

He was the first person who heard his son Joseph's testimony after he had seen the angel, and exhorted him to be faithful and diligent in obeying the instructions he had received. He was baptized April 6, 1830. Prior to this time he had become one of the Eight Witnesses of the Book of Mormon.

In August, 1830, in company with his son, Don Carlos, he took a mission to St. Lawrence County, New York, touching on his route at several of the

Canadian ports, where he distributed a few copies of the Book of Mormon, visited his father, brothers and sisters residing in St. Lawrence County, bore testimony to the truth, which resulted eventually in all the family coming into the Church, excepting his brother Jesse and sister Susan.

He removed with his family to Kirtland in 1831, was ordained Patriarch and president of the High Priesthood, under the hands of Joseph Smith, Oliver Cowdery, Sidney Rigdon and Frederick G. Williams, on December 18, 1833, and was a member of the first High Council, organized in Kirtland, Ohio, February 17, 1834.

In 1836 he traveled in company with his brother John, 2,400 miles in Ohio, New York, Pennsylvania, Vermont and New Hampshire, visiting the branches of the Church in those states, and bestowing Patriarchal blessings on several hundred persons, preaching the gospel to all who would hear, and baptizing many. They returned to Kirtland October 2, 1836.

During the persecutions in Kirtland, in 1837, he was made a prisoner, but fortunately obtained his liberty, and after a very tedious journey in the spring and summer of 1838, he arrived at Far West, Missouri. After his sons Hyrum and Joseph were thrown into the Missouri jails by the mob, he fled from under the exterminating order of Governor Lilburn W. Boggs, and made his escape in midwinter to Quincy, Illinois, from whence he removed to Commerce in the spring of 1839, and thus became one of the founders of Nauvoo.

The exposures he suffered brought on consumption, of which he died September 14, 1840, aged 69 years, two months and two days. He was 6 feet 2 inches tall, very straight, and remarkably well proportioned. His ordinary weight was about 200 pounds, and he was very strong and active. In his younger days he was famed as a wrestler. He was one of the most benevolent of men, opening his house to all who were destitute. While at Quincy, Illinois, he fed hundreds of the poor Saints who were fleeing from the Missouri persecutions, although he had arrived there penniless himself. (See *L. D. S. Biographical Encyclopedia*, vol. 1, p. 181)

VII

HYRUM SMITH

PATRIARCH OF THE whole Church and brother to
the Prophet Joseph, was born in Tunbridge, Vermont, February 9, 1800, and married Jerusha Bar-
den November 2, 1826, by whom he had six children:
Lovina, Mary, John, Hyrum, Jerusha and Sarah.
Hyrum's wife died on the 13th of October, 1837,
while he was absent at Far West, Missouri. He was
married to Mary Fielding the same year, by whom
he had two children, Joseph F. and Martha. Like
his brother Joseph, Hyrum spent his early years in
agricultural labors, and nothing of particular note
characterized that period of his life. He became a
believer in his brother Joseph's mission, and by him
was baptized in Seneca Lake, in June, 1829. He was
one of the eight persons permitted to view the plates
from which the Book of Mormon was translated, and
his name is prefixed to it as a witness. On November
7, 1837, at a conference assembled in Far West, Mo.,
he was appointed second counselor to President
Joseph Smith, instead of Frederick G. Williams, who
was rejected. On January 19, 1841, he was called
by revelation to take the office of Patriarch to the
whole Church, to which he had been appointed by
his deceased father, by blessing and also by birth-

right, and was likewise appointed a Prophet, Seer and Revelator. He was personally connected with many of the principal events of the Church, up to the time of his death, and in the various offices he filled, won the love and esteem of all persons. In the revelation calling him to be the chief Patriarch, the Lord thus spoke of him: "Blessed is my servant Hyrum Smith, for I the Lord love him, because of the integrity of his heart, and because he loveth that which is right before me, saith the Lord" (Doc. and Cov., 124:15). He was tenderly attached to his brother Joseph, whom he never left more than six months at one time during their lifetime. He was arrested with him at Far West, Mo., and imprisoned with him at Liberty, and finally was assassinated with him at Carthage, Ill., June 27, 1844. In this catastrophe he fell first, exclaiming, "I am a dead man," and Joseph responding, "O, dear brother Hyrum!"

In the *Times and Seasons* shortly after his death, there is the following beautiful eulogy: "He lived so far beyond the ordinary walk of man, that even the tongue of the vilest slanderer could not touch his reputation. He lived godly, and he died godly, and his murderers will yet have to confess that it would have been better for them to have had a mill-stone tied to them, and have been cast into the depths of the sea, and remain there while eternity goes and eternity comes, than to have robbed that noble man of heaven of his life." At his death he held various military and civil offices in the Nauvoo Legion and in the municipality.

In 1901, his son, Joseph F. Smith, became the sixth president of the Church. (*L. D. S. Biographical Encyclopedia*, vol. 1, p. 52)

VIII

SAMUEL HARRISON SMITH

THE FOURTH SON of Joseph Smith and Lucy Mack, was born in the town of Tunbridge, Orange County, Vermont, March 13, 1808. In his early life he assisted his father in farming. He possessed a religious turn of mind, and at an early age joined the Presbyterian Church, to which sect he belonged until he visited his brother Joseph in Pennsylvania in May, 1829, when Joseph informed him that the Lord was about to commence his latter-day work. He also showed him that part of the Book of Mormon which he had translated, and labored to persuade him concerning the gospel of Jesus Christ, which was about to be revealed in its fulness.

Samuel was not, however, very easily persuaded of these things, but after much inquiry and explanation he retired and prayed that he might obtain from the Lord wisdom to enable him to judge for himself; the result was that he obtained revelation for himself sufficient to convince him of the truth of the testimony of his brother Joseph.

May 15, 1829, Joseph Smith and Oliver Cowdery were baptized, and as they were returning from the river to the house, they overheard Samuel engaged in secret prayer. Joseph said that he considered that a sufficient testimony of his being a fit subject for baptism; and as they had now received authority to baptize, they spoke to Samuel upon the subject, and he went straightway to the water with them, and was baptized by Oliver Cowdery, he being the third person baptized in the last dispensation. A short time later he became one of the Eight Witnesses of the Book of Mormon.

Samuel was present at the organization of the Church, April 6, 1830, and was one of the six who at that time constituted the first members of the Church. He was ordained to the Priesthood on that day.

On the 30th of June following the organization of the Church, Samuel took some Books of Mormon and started on his mission, to which he had been set apart by his brother Joseph, and on traveling twenty-five miles, which was his first day's journey, he stopped at a number of places in order to sell his books, but was turned out of doors as soon as he declared his principles.

In December, 1830, Samuel was sent to preach in Kirtland, Ohio, and the surrounding country. In the beginning of 1831, Joseph, the Prophet, moved to Kirtland to preside, accompanied by Hyrum and many of the Saints, and soon after his father's family and the Saints who were located in Fayette, near Waterloo, also moved to Kirtland.

In June, 1831, Samuel was called by revelation

to go to Missouri on a mission, in company with Reynolds Cahoon.

When they started for Missouri, about fifty brethren set out for the same place, and when they all arrived they met on the spot selected for the Temple, in Jackson County.

Brothers Smith and Cahoon spent several days in Jackson County, attended conferences, and were with Joseph when he received several revelations. While in Missouri they were requested to remain together on their mission until they reached home, which was in September following.

Soon after their arrival in Kirtland, they took a mission into the southern townships and counties of Ohio. Brother Cahoon returned after laboring about six weeks, but Samuel continued preaching through the winter, strengthening the churches and comforting the Saints.

In a revelation given in January, 1832, Orson Hyde and Samuel H. Smith were called to go on a mission to the Eastern country; accordingly they started in March, and traveled and preached the gospel through the states of Ohio, New York, Pennsylvania, Connecticut, Rhode Island, Massachusetts and Maine. They returned to Kirtland in December.

February 17, 1834, Samuel was ordained and set apart as one of the High Council in Kirtland, in which office he officiated until he went to Missouri in 1838.

On August 13, 1834, Samuel married Mary Bailey, who was born in Bedford, Hillsborough County, New Hampshire, December 20, 1808.

In 1838 he traveled in company with his brother Joseph from Kirtland to Missouri. He passed through the mobbings of that year, in Far West and Adam-ondi-Ahman, Missouri, and his family suffered from exposure as they were driven out of the state by the mob.

Samuel arrived in Quincy, and was there to assist his father and mother over the river on their arrival. He rented a house for them, into which he also assisted four other families of the Saints.

Samuel's wife died January 25, 1841. She was the mother of four children, namely: Susannah B., Mary B., Samuel Harrison B. and Lucy B.

In April, 1841, he was sent on a mission to preach the gospel in Scott and adjoining counties, Illinois. May 3rd, he married Levira Clark, daughter of Gardner and Delecta Clark, born in Livonia, Livingston County, New York, July 30, 1815.

In the month of November he returned to Nauvoo, taking his family with him, where he remained during the winter, and also the summer of 1842, during which time he worked mostly for Joseph, and harvested in the country.

In the fall of 1842 Samuel removed to his brother William's tavern at Plymouth. In the summer of 1843 he was often at Nauvoo. In the fall he chopped wood, and prepared his farm by making fences and clearing off the timber, preaching the gospel in the vicinity as he had the opportunity.

In the spring of 1844 he cultivated his farm, and in June, having heard of the imprisonment of his brothers in Carthage jail, he repaired thither on horseback to see them. While on the way he was pursued by the mobocrats; but in consequence of the fleetness of his horse, he was enabled to reach Carthage shortly after the tragedy. The following day he went to Nauvoo in company with the bodies of his martyred brothers.

About two weeks after the death of his brothers, Samuel suffered a severe illness and died on the 30th of July, 1844, aged 36 years.

The following extract is from his obituary notice, published in the *Times and Seasons*:

"The exit of this worthy man, so soon after the horrible butchery of his brothers, Joseph and Hyrum, in Carthage jail, is a matter of deep solemnity to the family, as well as a remediless loss to all. If ever there lived a good man upon the earth, Samuel H. Smith was that person. His labors in the Church from first to last, carrying glad tidings to the eastern cities, and finally his steadfastness as one of the witnesses to the Book of Mormon, and many saintly traits of virtue, knowledge, temperance, patience, godliness, brotherly kindness, and charity, shall be given of him hereafter, as a man of God." (From sketch written by Andrew Jenson. *L. D. S. Biographical Encyclopedia*, vol. 1, p. 278)

Part Six

★ ★ ★ ★

MISCELLANEOUS DOCUMENTS

I

STATEMENT OF PRESIDENT BRIGHAM YOUNG REGARDING THE PLATES OF THE BOOK OF MORMON

The following informative statement was made by President Young as part of a public address at Farmington, Utah, on June 17, 1877, some two months prior to his death. It is found in the Journal of Discourses, vol. 19, p. 38.

I COULD RELATE many very singular circumstances. I lived right in the country where the plates were found from which the Book of Mormon was translated, and I know a great many things pertaining to that country. I believe I will take the liberty to tell you of another circumstance that will be as marvelous as anything can be. This is an incident in the life of Oliver Cowdery, but he did not take the liberty of telling such things in meeting as I take. I tell these things to you, and I have a motive for doing so. I want to carry them to the ears of my brethren and sisters, and to the children also, that they may grow to an understanding of some things that seem to be entirely hidden from the human family. Oliver Cowdery went with the Prophet Joseph when he deposited these plates. Joseph did not translate all of the plates; there was a portion of them sealed, which you can learn from the Book of Doctrine and Covenants. When Joseph got the plates, the angel instructed him to carry them back to the hill Cumorah, which he did. Oliver says that when Joseph and Oliver went there, the hill opened, and they walked into a cave, in which there was a large and spacious room. He says he did not think, at the time, whether they had the light of the sun or artificial light; but that it was just as light as day. They laid the plates on a table; it was a large table that stood in the room. Under this table there was a pile of plates as much as two feet high, and there were altogether in this room more plates than, probably, many wagon loads; they were piled up in the corners and along the walls. The first time they went there the sword of Laban hung upon the wall; but when they went again it had been taken down and laid upon the table across the gold plates — it was unsheathed, and on it was written these words: "This sword will never be sheathed again until the kingdoms of this world become the kingdom of our God and His Christ." I tell you this as coming not only from Oliver Cowdery, but others who were familiar with it, and who understood it just as well as we understand coming to this meeting, enjoying the day, and by and by we separate and go away, forgetting most of what is said, but remembering some things. So is it with other circumstances in life. I relate this to you, and I want you to under-

[174]

stand it. I take this liberty of referring to those things so that they will not be forgotten and lost. Carlos Smith was a young man of as much veracity as any young man we had, and he was a witness to these things. Samuel Smith saw some things, Hyrum saw a good many things, but Joseph was the leader.

II

STATEMENT OF JOHN WHITMER

John Whitmer was one of the Eight Witnesses of the Book of Mormon. He lived in Kirtland during 1835 and 1836, and for a time was employed as editor of the "Messenger and Advocate," the official Church publication. In March 1836 he resigned from this position and wrote an article stating he was retiring from the editorial department. In the article the following paragraph appeared. It is found in the March 1836 number of the paper, pages 236-237. He reiterates his testimony of the Book of Mormon.

To the patrons of the Latter-day Saints Messenger and Advocate:

It may not be amiss to give a statement to the world, concerning the work of the Lord, as I have been a member of this Church of Latter-day Saints from its beginning.

To say that the Book of Mormon is a revelation from God I have no hesitancy, but with all confidence have signed my name to it as such; and I hope that my patrons will indulge me, in speaking freely on this subject, as I am about leaving the editorial department — Therefore I desire to testify to all that will come to a knowledge of this address, that I have most assuredly seen the plates from whence the Book of Mormon is translated, and I have handled these plates, and know of a surety that Joseph Smith, Jr., has translated the Book by the gift and power of God, and in this thing the wisdom of the wise most assuredly has perished.

(Signed) John Whitmer.

III

VISIT OF GEORGE Q. CANNON
TO DAVID WHITMER

During the pioneer period of Utah, George Q. Cannon was one of the leaders of the Latter-day Saints. He came to Salt Lake Valley in 1847; was ordained an Apostle in 1860. In 1872 he was elected to Congress and served for ten years. He was counselor to three presidents of the Church. The visit to David Whitmer occurred in 1884 and George Q. Cannon wrote the following account, which appeared in the Juvenile Instructor, vol. 19, p. 106.

ON MY RETURN from my visit to the east I took the opportunity of calling at Richmond, Ray County, Missouri, to see the last surviving witness of the three to whom the angel exhibited the plates of the Book of Mormon—David Whitmer.

From Kansas City I took train for Lexington Junction, and there changed cars for Richmond. Upon arriving at the station I inquired of a gentleman who was standing there if he knew Mr. Whitmer. He told me that his son, David J. Whitmer, would be there presently, as he owned the omnibus which carried passengers from the station to the hotels. In a short time the omnibus drove up, and the gentleman of whom I had made the inquiry pointed Mr. Whitmer out to me. I found him very courteous, and upon informing him who I was he appeared to have been expecting me, having heard through some of the papers that I was intending to make such a visit. He said his father was growing very feeble and he did not like to have him interviewed, but he would arrange for me to see him as soon as he could.

I drove to the hotel, and after dinner Mr. Whitmer called upon me and conducted me to the residence of his father. On the way there he pointed out the track of a cyclone which had visited the town in 1878, and which had left their house, or rather the room in which the mansucript of the Book of Mormon was kept, in such a condition as to astonish all the people. The roof of the house was blown off; but nothing in this room was disturbed. The glass was not even broken. This was a cause of astonishment to the neighborhood, and the family evidently ascribe the protection of the room and its contents to the fact of the manuscript being there.

David Whitmer, who was born in January, 1805, is growing feeble, but his mind is bright and apparently unimpaired. He is rather slender now and probably stood in his early manhood five feet ten or perhaps five feet eleven inches in height. I noticed in shaking hands with him that the thumb of his right hand is missing and the hand has a long scar in the center from some injury that he had received. His hair is thin and he is rather bald. His nose is aquiline; his eyes black, or a dark brown. I noticed a slight German accent or tone in his talk. The Whitmer family is of German origin, his mother, I believe, having been born on the Rhine. He has evidently been a man who in his prime must have been quite interesting, and, I should think, fine looking. I was shown a likeness of his, painted in oil, when he was thirty-two years old. This makes him appear as handsome, of marked features, rather Jewish looking, with a head of thick hair inclined to curl.

After some little conversation he inquired of me if I would like to see the manuscript, and gave his son a key and told him to bring it in. I found it wonderfully well preserved, written in different handwritings. He says they are the writings of Oliver Cowdery, Emma Smith, Martin Harris, and perhaps, some of it that of his brother Christian, who assisted the Prophet Joseph. This is the manuscript, Mr. Whitmer says, from which the printers set the type of the Book of Mormon, and he pointed out to me where it had been cut for conveniences as "copy." I noticed some printer's marks on the manuscript. Still it seemed unusually clean for "copy" that printers had handled. I commented upon the cleanness of the manuscript and he explained that it was in consequence of the care taken of it by Oliver Cowdery in watching it while in the printer's hands. It was fastened together, not as a whole, but a few sheets—probably not more than a dozen—with woolen yarn, which he said was his mother's. I examined this manuscript with great interest and with a feeling of reverence. How many associations cluster around this! What wonderful changes have occurred since the few who were interested in this work labored in its preparation under the direction of the Prophet! Everything connected with the work then was in the future. Their minds were filled with anticipation concerning the greatness of the work, the foundation of which they were assisting to lay. But how little conception after all, probably, these men had, with the exception of Joseph, of the wonderful character of the work to be accomplished. Thoughts like these passed through my mind while looking at this manuscript.

But there was a paper with this, which, if anything, was still more interesting than the manuscript. It was the characters drawn by Joseph himself from the plates for Martin Harris to take to show the learned professors, so wonderfully predicted in the 29th chapter of Isaiah. There were seven lines of these characters, the first four being about twice as large in size as the last three. In English Joseph had written over the lines the word "characters." He had spelled this word, "caractors." Though these characters had evidently been written for a long time, they were as clear and distinct as though just penned. Here was the very paper which Isaiah saw in vision about 2,600 years before, and which he called "the words of a book." How wonderfully God in His own way brings to pass the fulfillment of the predictions of his servants! To the ordinary person it might seem like a trifling thing to copy these characters and send them "to one that is learned;" but it was of sufficient importance in the mind of the Lord for him to inspire his servant Isaiah to describe exactly the occurrence. This shows how much importance the Lord attached to these details connected with the foundation of this work and the coming forth of the Book of Mormon.

David Whitmer told me he was plowing when Joseph and Oliver came to him to speak about his being one of the witnesses. He already knew that the Lord had promised to show the plates to three witnesses. Joseph then informed him that he was chosen to be one of the three. They went out and sat upon a log, conversing upon the things to be revealed, when they were surrounded by a glorious light which overshadowed them. A glorious personage appeared unto them and exhibited to them the plates, the sword of Laban, the Directors which were given to Lehi (called Liahona), the Urim and Thummim, and other records. Human language cannot, he said, describe what they saw. He had had his hours of darkness and trial and difficulty since that period; but however dark upon other things his mind had been, that vision had ever been a bright and beautiful scene in his memory, and he had never wavered in regard to it. He had fearlessly testified of it always, even when his life was threatened. Martin Harris was not with them at the time Joseph and Oliver and he saw the angel; but he and Joseph afterwards were together, and the angel exhibited the plates to Martin Harris also, and he thus became a witness.

I spent several hours there, and to me they were very interesting. The old gentleman was able to stay in the room only a portion of the time; he had to retire to rest; but I had the company of his son, David J. Whitmer, and his nephew, John C. Whitmer (who is a son of Jacob Whitmer, one of the eight witnesses to the Book of Mormon), while I remained.

The old jail in which the Prophet Joseph and other brethren were imprisoned at Richmond had long ago disappeared; a brick one had been built in its stead, and it had passed away, having been replaced by a stone building which now stands. The town contains, I was informed, about 3,500 inhabitants, including coal miners, of whom there are a large number, there being good coal found here. I was not favorably impressed with the appearance of the country and improvements. There is not much enterprise shown, and the buildings are not of a superior kind. I have no doubt the soil is rich and produces plentifully, but there seems to be very little push among the people.

—*Juvenile Instructor,* vol. 19, p. 106.

IV

STATEMENT OF ORSON PRATT REGARD-
ING THE WITNESSES OF THE
BOOK OF MORMON

Orson Pratt was baptized in the fall of 1830, the year in which the Church was organized and in which the Book of Mormon was printed. He was personally acquainted with the Prophet Joseph Smith and with all the Witnesses of the Book of Mormon. His observations should therefore be of interest and significance to students of Church history. The following remarks are from a sermon he delivered in 1877 and are found in the Journal of Discourses, vol. 18, pp. 156-161.

IN THE FIRST place, I will give you a very brief statement concerning the manner in which the Book of Mormon was found. In the year 1827, a young man, a farmer's boy by the name of Joseph Smith, was visited by an holy angel, as he had been for several years prior to this time. But on this occasion, in the fall of 1827, he was permitted to take into his possession the plates from which the Book of Mormon was translated — the angel gave them into his hands, permitted him to take them from the place of their deposit, and they were delivered to Mr. Smith by the angel of God. With this book, called the Book of Mormon, was a very curious instrument, such a one, probably, as no person had seen for many generations; it was called by the angel of God, the Urim and Thummim. We know that such an instrument existed in ancient times among the Jews and among the Israelites in the wilderness, and that it was used to inquire of the Lord. So sacred was that instrument in the days of Moses, that Aaron, the chief priest of the whole house of Israel, was commanded to place it within his breastplate, that when he should judge the tribes of the house of Israel, he should not judge by his own wisdom, but should inquire of the Lord by means of this instrument, and whatever decision the Lord, by aid of the Urim and Thummim, should give, all Israel should give heed to it. The same instrument was in use, many hundred years after the days of Aaron, by the Prophets of Israel. David inquired, by means of an instrument of that kind, concerning his enemies (who pursued him from city to city), asking the Lord certain questions — whether his enemies would come to the city where he happened to be, and whether he would be delivered up to them by the people of that city— and the Lord gave him all the necessary instruction, and by this means he was delivered out of the hands of his enemies from time to time.

But it seems that, before the coming of Christ, for some reason, probably through wickedness, the Urim and Thummim were taken away from the children of Israel, and a prophecy was uttered by one of the ancient Prophets, before Christ, that they should be many days without a Priest, without the Urim and Thummim, without the ephod, and without many things that God blessed them with in the days of their righteousness; but that in the latter days God would again restore all his blessings to the people of Israel, including their counselors and their judges as at the first.

With these plates that Joseph Smith, the Prophet, obtained through the instructions of the angel, he also obtained the Urim and Thummim, and by their aid he copied a few characters from the plates and translated them. He was not a learned man himself, but an ignorant farmer's boy, scarcely having the first rudiments of an education. He could read and write a little, and that was about the amount of his educational acquirements. After having copied a few of the characters from these plates and translating them, he committed them into the hands of Martin Harris, a man with whom he was acquainted, who lived not far from his neighborhood. Martin Harris took these few characters and their translation to the city of New York to show them to the learned and, if possible, to get some information in regard to their meaning. This was in the year 1827. Martin Harris was then a middle-aged man, being about forty-six years of age. On arriving in New York City, he visited the learned Dr. Mitchell, professor of languages, and obtained some information from him in relation to the manuscript which he held, and was recommended by Dr. Mitchell to see Mr. Anthon, professor of ancient and modern languages —probably one of the most learned men in ancient languages that ever lived in our nation. Mr. Harris went to see Mr. Anthon and showed him the characters. The professor examined them and the translation and, according to the testimony of Martin Harris given from this stand, he gave him a certificate that, so far as he could understand the characters, the translation seemed to be correct; but he wished further time and desired that the original plates should be brought to him. Mr. Harris then informed him how Mr. Smith came in possession of the plates — that he did not find them accidentally, but that an angel of God revealed to him the place of their deposit. This was after Martin Harris had obtained the certificate from Professor Anthon, and just before Mr. Harris took his leave of the learned gentleman. The latter, having ascertained how Mr. Smith came in possession of the plates — that part of them were sealed, and that the Lord had given a strict command that they should not be shown to the public, but only to certain witnesses—I say that the professor, having learned this, wished to see the certificate again. Mr. Harris returned it to him, and he tore it up, saying that there was no such thing as angels, or communications from the Lord in our day; and upon Mr. Harris' telling him that a portion of the plates were sealed, he very sarcastically remarked that he could not read a sealed book.

[187]

Mr. Harris left him, and returned some two hundred and fifty miles or more to the neighborhood where the plates were found, and informed Mr. Smith of his success with the learned; after which the Lord gave a special command to Joseph, unlearned as he was, that he should translate the record by the aid of the Urim and Thummim. Mr. Smith commenced the work of translation. Mr. Harris, acting as his scribe, wrote from his mouth one hundred and sixteen pages of the first translation, given by the Prophet.

The work was continued from time to time, until finally the unsealed portion of the Book of Mormon was all translated. In the meantime Martin Harris, Joseph Smith (the translator of the book), Oliver Cowdery and David Whitmer (four persons) retired to a little grove—in the year 1829—not far from the house of old father Whitmer, where this Church was organized. They retired to this grove for the special purpose of calling on the name of the Lord, and they all knelt down and commenced praying, one by one, and while thus engaged they saw an angel of God descend from the heavens, very bright and glorious in his appearance; and he came and stood in their midst, and he took the plates and turned over leaf after leaf of the unsealed portion, and showed to these four men the engravings upon them; and at the same time they heard a voice out of heaven saying unto them that the plates had been translated correctly and commanding them to bear testimony of the same to all nations, kindreds, tongues and people to whom the translation should be sent. In accordance with this command, Oliver Cowdery, David Whitmer and Martin Harris have attached their testimony after the title page of the Book of Mormon, testifying to the appearance of the angel, signing their names and testifying to the correctness of the translation — testifying to having seen the plates and the engravings upon them, and to the voice of the Lord, which they heard out of the heavens.

Now let me say a few words concerning the nature of this testimony. This testimony was given prior to the publication of the book and also previous to the organization of the Latter-day Saint Church. The book was printed early in 1830, with their testimony. Thus you perceive that this work, this marvelous work, was not presented to the inhabitants of the earth for their belief until God had favored them with four persons who could bear witness to what their eyes had seen, what their ears had heard, and what their hands had handled. Consequently there was no possibility, so far as these four men were concerned, that they themselves could be deceived. It would be impossible for four men to be together and all of them to be deceived in seeing an angel descend from heaven, and in regard to the brightness of his countenance and the glory of his person, hearing his voice, and seeing him lay his hands upon one of them, namely David Whitmer, and speaking these words: "Blessed be the Lord and they who keep His commandments." After seeing the plates, the engravings upon them, and the angel, and hearing the voice of the Lord out of heaven, every person will say that there was no possibility of either of these men being deceived in relation to this matter. In other words, if it were to be maintained that in their case it was an hallucination of the brain and that they were deceived, then with the same propriety might it be asserted that all other men, in every age, who profess to have seen angels, were also deceived—and this might be applied to the Prophets, Patriarchs, Apostles, and others who lived in ancient times, who declared they saw angels, as well as to Oliver Cowdery, Martin Harris, and David Whitmer. But, says the objector, "No, those who testify that they saw angels anciently were not deceived, but they who come testifying about such ministrations in the latter days may be deceived." Now let me ask, is there anything logical in such reasoning as this? If these, in the latter days, who testify to having seen angels, were deceived, all who testify to the same things in former days might have been deceived on the same grounds. And then, if these men, whose testimonies are attached to the Book of Mormon, were not deceived, it must be admitted that they were impostors of the most barefaced character, or else that the Book of Mormon is a divine record sent from heaven; one or the other must be admitted — there is no halfway in the matter. If they were not deceived — which they could not possibly have been according to the very nature of their testimony—then there are only two alternatives: they were impostors, or else the Book of Mormon is a divine revelation from heaven.

Now let us inquire what grounds there are to suppose that they were impostors. Forty-six years have passed away since this angel appeared and showed the plates to these individuals. Has anything transpired during this time that would give us any grounds to suppose that they were impostors? For instance, has either of these witnesses, or the translator of the engravings on the plates, ever, under any circumstances, denied his testimony? No. We have some accounts in the Bible of men of God, some of the greatest men that lived in ancient times, denying the things of God. We read of Peter cursing and swearing that he never knew Jesus, and yet he was one of the foremost of the Apostles. His testimony was true so far as seeing and being acquainted with Jesus was concerned, and in regard to the divinity of Jesus. Why? Because God had revealed it to him and yet he denied it. "Blessed art thou, Simon Barjonah," said Jesus, speaking to Peter, "for flesh and blood have not revealed this unto thee, but my Father who is in heaven." Peter knew, just as well as he knew that he had a being, that Jesus was the son of God; it had been revealed to him from the heavens, and though he afterwards, through fear, in the presence of the high priest, cursed and swore and denied it, yet the former testimony that he had given was true.

Now did either of these three men, or did the translator of the Book of Mormon, ever deny the truth, as Peter did? Did they ever in any way deny the divinity of the Book of Mormon? Never, no never. Whatever the circumstances they were placed in, however much they were mobbed and ridiculed, however much they suffered by the persecution of their enemies, their testimony all the time was: "We saw the angel of God, we beheld him in his glory, we saw the plates in his hands, and the engravings thereon, and we know that the Book of Mormon is true." Joseph Smith continued to bear this testimony until the day of his death; he sealed his testimony as a martyr in this Church, being shot down by his enemies, who were blackened up and disguised, in order that they might not be known. Oliver Cowdery did not live his faith as he should have done, and he was excommunicated from this Church during Joseph's lifetime. Did he still continue to hold fast to his testimony? He did. Never was he known to swerve from it in the least degree; and after being out of the Church several years, he returned to Council Bluffs, where there was a branch of the Church, and at a conference he acknowledged his sins and humbly asked the Church to forgive him, bearing his testimony to the sacred things recorded in the Book of Mormon—that he saw the angel and the plates, just according to the testimony to which he had appended his name. He was rebaptized a member of the Church, and soon after departed this life.

Martin Harris did not follow up this people to the State of Missouri, neither did he follow us up to the State of Illinois; but we often heard of him, and whenever we did so, we heard of him telling in public and in private of the great vision that God had shown to him concerning the divinity of the Book of Mormon. A few years ago he came to this territory, an old man between eighty and ninety years of age, and spoke from this stand, in the hearing of the people. He then located himself in Cache County, in the northern part of the Territory, where he continued to live until last Saturday, when he departed this life in his ninety-third year—a good old age. Did he continue to bear testimony all that length of time—over forty-six years of life? Did he, at any time during that long period, waver in the least degree from his testimony? Not at all. He had a great many follies and imperfections, like all other people, like the ancient Apostles, like Elijah the Prophet, but after all, he continued to testify to the very last concerning the truth of this work. Nothing seemed to delight him so much as to tell about the angel and the plates that he had seen. It was only a short time prior to his death that one of our bishops went in to see the old man. His pulse was apparently sluggish in its movements and nearly gone, but the sight of the bishop seemed to revive him, and he said to him—"I am going." The bishop related to him some things which he thought would be interesting, among them that the Book of Mormon had been translated into the Spanish language for the benefit of a great many of the descendants of Israel in this country, who understand the Spanish language (in Mexico and Central America). This intelligence seemed to revive the old man, and he began to talk about the Book of Mormon. New strength, apparently, was imparted to him, and he continued his conversation for some two hours; and in his last testimony he bore record concerning the divinity of the work, and was rejoiced to think that it was going forth in another language, that those who understood that language might be made acquainted with the wonderful works of God.

I will here state that Martin Harris, when he came to this Territory a few years ago, was rebaptized, the same as every member of the Church from distant parts is on arriving here. That seems to be a kind of standing ordinance for all Latter-day Saints who emigrate here, from the First Presidency down; all are rebaptized and set out anew by renewing their covenants. There are thousands of Latter-day Saints who have gone forth into the baptismal font, and been baptized for their dead kindred and friends. Martin Harris requested this privilege, and he was baptized here in Salt Lake City for many of his kindred who are dead. I mention these things in order that the Saints may understand something concerning this man who has just left us, almost a hundred years old. God favored him, highly favored him. He was among the favored few who went up from the state of Ohio in the summer of 1831, and journeyed nearly a thousand miles to the western part of Missouri, to Jackson County. The Prophet went at the same time, and that was designated as the land where the Saints should eventually be gathered, and where a great city should be eventually reared, called the city of Zion or the New Jerusalem, and that the Saints should be located throughout all that region of country. God gave many commandments in those days concerning what might be termed the United Order; in other words, concerning the consecration of the properties of the Church. These things were given by revelation through the Prophet. Martin Harris was the first man that the Lord called by name to consecrate his money and lay the same at the feet of the Bishop in Jackson County, Missouri, according to the order of consecration. He willingly did it; he knew the work to be true; he knew that the word of the Lord through the Prophet Joseph was just as sacred as any word that ever came from the mouth of any Prophet from the foundation of the world. He consecrated his money and his substance, according to the word of the Lord. What for? As the revelation states, as an example to the rest of the Church.

As I have already mentioned, one more witness remains who saw that angel and the plates. Who is it? David Whitmer, a younger man than Martin Harris, probably some seventy years of age—I do not recollect his age exactly. Where does he live? In the western part of Missouri. Does he still hold fast to his testimony? He does. Many of the Elders of this

[195]

Church, in going to and fro among the nations, have called upon him from time to time, and they all bear the same testimony—that Mr. David Whitmer still, in the most solemn manner, declares that he saw the angel and that he saw the plates in his hands. But he is not here with us; he has not gathered up with the people of God. That, however, does not prove that his testimony is not true, by any means.

Index

INDEX

American Encyclopedia, 100

Anthon, Charles, visited by Martin Harris, 108

Apostles chosen, 39

Babel, Tower of, 22

Baptism, 35

Bidamon, Emma Hale Smith, 26

Bidamon, Major, 28

Book of Mormon: revelation pertaining to three witnesses, 3; passages in same pertaining to witnesses, 5, 12; eleven witnesses testify of, 24; written by Oliver Cowdery, 47; manuscript of, described, 73; David Whitmer, last surviving witness of, 76; Martin Harris mortgages farm to pay for publication of, 109; plates of Book of Mormon deposited in Hill Cumorah, 173

Brass Plates, 68

Cannon, George Q., 178

Council Bluffs, 41

Cowdery, Oliver: one of three witnesses, 5; revelation to, 6; testimony of, 9; sketch of life, 33; bears testimony in Michigan, 45; returns to Church, 47; rebaptized, 50; heard by Edward Stevenson, 51; last testimony of, 55; death of, 57

Cumorah, hill, 70

Davis, Congressman, 25

Des Moines, Ia., 128

Dille, David B., 112

Doniphan, A. W., 90

Encyclopedia Britannica, 100

Evening and Morning Star, 38

First vision described, 19

Harmony, Pa., 34, 69

Harris, Martin: one of witnesses, 5; revelation to, 6; sees vision, 9; testimony of, 9; sketch of life, 107; testimony of, to David B. Dille, 112; testimony of, to William H. Homer, 115; visited by Edward Stevenson, 124; arrival in Salt Lake, 129; rebaptized, 132; death of, 142

Homer, William H., 115

Independence, Mo., 37

Jackson County, 85

Jaredites, 22

Jerusalem, 22

Johnson, Luke, 24

Jolly, Julia A., 63

Kanesville, Ia., 47

Kansas City Journal, 75

Laban, sword of, 68

Lehi, Book of, 81

Manchester, N. Y., 18, 33

Manuscript of Book of Mormon, 72

Melchizedek Priesthood, 35

Michigan, 43

Moyle, James H., 92

Nephites, the three, 71

Nielsen, Judge C. M., 42

Orange, Ohio, 24

Page, Hiram, 155

Pratt, Orson, 65, 176, 177

Pratt, Parley P., 37

Priesthood of Aaron, 35

Reorganized Church, 26

Richards, Samuel W., 52

Rigdon, Sidney, 96

Sacred Record, 34

Savior appeared on this continent, 22

[199]